Drawn Fabric Embroidery

Drawn Fabric Embroidery

Agnes M. Leach

DOVER PUBLICATIONS, INC.
Mineola, New York

Bibliographical Note

This Dover edition, first published in 2001, is a slightly revised republication of the work originally published in 1959 by E. Hulton and Company, Limited, London.

The only significant alteration consists of omitting the text from the original page 114 of the 1959 edition—"Addresses Where Materials Are Available"—since the list provided therein is unlikely to be of much practical use today. While the *specific* materials listed on page 13 of the book may not now be as readily available as they were in 1959 when the original edition was published, the enterprising reader will undoubtedly find viable substitutes.

Library of Congress Cataloging-in-Publication Data

Leach, Agnes M.
    Drawn fabric embroidery / Agnes M. Leach.
        p. cm.
    Reprint. Originally published: London : E. Hulton, 1959.
    ISBN 0-486-41809-X (pbk.)
        1. Drawn-work. I. Title.

TT785 .L43 2001
746.44—dc21

2001028700

Manufactured in the United States by Courier Corporation
41809X02
www.doverpublications.com

CONTENTS

List of
Illustrations

FOREWORD

Counted thread embroidery, deriving from peasant origins, remains to this day the embroidery of the ordinary folk. There is nothing esoteric about it; it is well within the ability of any average needlewoman who can count and who will take the trouble to be meticulously accurate. The more elaborate forms demand some degree of artistry and skill, and amongst these Drawn Fabric holds the highest place, offering to the worker the widest scope for her imagination and enabling her to give free rein to her fancy.

In compiling this book, I have been helped by many friends, who have read parts of it, have made comments or suggestions or who have patiently listened whilst I meditated aloud. To all of them I offer my sincere thanks. I am also grateful to Mrs. van Wyk for permission to reproduce her beautiful cloth, to Fru Gertie Wandel of Haandarbejdets Fremme, Copenhagen, for permission to include some hitherto unpublished details of the buttonhole picot edging illustrated in Fig. 108, to Miss E. M. Clark for allowing me to show her own variation of the edging illustrated in Fig. 109, and to Mrs. Nancy Evans for sparing time to read the whole book. My principal debt is to the Embroiderers' Guild, whose resources have been placed at my disposal, and to the Secretary, Miss Sinclair Salmon, whose encouragement emboldened me to undertake this task, and who, by her unflagging enthusiasm has provided the stimulus which carried it to completion. I am particularly grateful to Miss Janet Boswell and Mrs. Phillis Groves for their help with the drawings.

This book makes no claim to be the last word on Drawn Fabric; that will never be said as long as this embroidery continues to be practised and discussed. But if it serves to introduce this fascinating work to those who have not yet attempted it, and to give some fresh ideas to those who already have some experience of it, I shall be well content.

Edinburgh   AGNES M. LEACH

CHAPTER I

Introduction

Drawn fabric embroidery, or pulled work as it is often popularly termed, is so frequently confused with drawn thread work, that it may be helpful at the outset to explain the distinction between them. In drawn thread work, threads lying in one direction are removed from the fabric to a depth of a half to two inches or more, and those lying in the other direction which are thus left exposed are then grouped, twisted or worked on to form more or less elaborate patterns. Unless the work is deliberately planned as a reinforcement to replace the missing threads and not merely for decoration, it remains inherently weak, and sooner or later it will give way, while the fabric itself is still sound. Drawn thread was very popular in Victorian and Edwardian times, but its fragility has caused it to fall out of favour. In drawn fabric, on the contrary, the material is left intact, but the threads are pulled apart or drawn together by stitchery in such a way that the holes left form a variety of patterns. Thus the material far from being weakened, is actually strengthened, and the work is as durable as the fabric on which it is done.

In its simplest from drawn fabric is an early development of embroidery, and peasant work of various types was done in many countries, ranging from Scandinavia to the Greek Islands. The Greek and Near Eastern work is unique in being done in thread of one or more colours contrasting with the material; elsewhere a matching thread was normally used. A piece of eighteenth century Danish peasant-work in the Victoria and Albert Museum, showing simple leaf shapes worked in a single filling and outlined in chain stitch on hand-woven linen, bears a striking resemblance to some modern Danish work; but the same century also produced the most elaborate and sophisticated examples of this embroidery, mainly French, Danish, German or Flemish. Worked on the sheerest cambric in floral designs of great beauty with a variety of fillings, and closely resembling the needlepoint lace of the period, it was used for ruffles, frills and lappets, and its resemblance to lace earned it the name of 'Dresden Point'. Many Museums, both in this country and abroad, have choice specimens, so fine that it seems scarcely possible that they could have been worked by the thread; the exactness of the stitchery as revealed by a magnifying glass testifies to the skill and the eyesight of our ancestors. It is worth recording that an attempt to introduce this work as an industry into Scotland at the end of the eighteenth century failed because the fine cambric which was required could not be imported from the Continent owing to the blockade during the Napoleonic Wars. Cotton was beginning to come from America, so the workers turned to muslin, adapted their designs and technique to the new material, and thus developed Ayrshire work, which is still so greatly admired and treasured in Scottish families.

In contrast with the lace-like cambric embroidery, drawn fabric was also used on linen for large panels, coverlets and gentlemen's waistcoats. Though on a larger scale and therefore coarser and heavier, the work shows the same beauty of design and stichery, and the same exactness of technique. It was occasionally used with corded quilting, the quilting being done on two thicknesses of linen. When this part of the work was completed, one thickness of linen was carefully cut out where open fillings were required, and drawn fabric stitches were worked on the linen that remained. In this heavier type of work, as the linen was closely woven, it was usual to draw out single threads at intervals to make the working easier.

The interest in drawn fabric appears to have waned somewhat during the nineteenth century, though it is too fundamental ever to die out completely, and it continued to be worked on the Continent. In the early years of this century interest revived once more in this country, receiving a strong impetus from Mrs. Newall, who did much research into materials and stitches, introduced the work to a wider public and started a cottage industry at Fisherton-de-la-Mere. Since then enthusiasm has gained momentum till today it amounts almost to a craze, and there can be few districts where classes are not eagerly attended and the work assiduously practised. It is being constantly developed on the Continent, too, notably in Denmark, Sweden and Switzerland, and new stitches or fresh arrangements of familiar ones are constantly being invented and devised. Not all of them are to be recommended unless the work is meant to be framed and used as wall decoration, for, though attractive in appearance, long threads lying at the back of the work make some of them impractical. It should always be remembered that this is essentially a practical form of embroidery, strong enough to stand up to daily use and regular laundering. Table and household linen, bed covers, cushion covers, tea-cosies and lampshades may all be decorated with it, provided that suitable stitches are used.

It will be readily understood that in the face of this constant and ever-increasing development, no book on the subject can claim to be exhaustive. All that can be done is to describe the various stitches, suggest how they may be combined and adapted, and offer hints on their use for practical purposes. Workers will very soon find that they are devising new schemes of stitchery for themselves.

CHAPTER II

Practical information

(a) Design

Drawn fabric designs are of two types. The first is geometrical and is based on the stitches themselves, which are built up to form abstract shapes, often connected by lines, broad or narrow. It depends for its effect on contrast, balance and proportion and the designs may be quite simple or very elaborate. Beginners usually find this the easier type to start on, since a few simple stitches can be combined to give a satisfying result, and even first efforts have a good chance of being successful. Success begets confidence, and confidence ambition to tackle something more advanced. Sometimes these abstract shapes suggest conventional natural forms, such as flowers, leaves, etc., similar to those found in the coloured embroideries of the Balkans and the Near East, and thus a more representational design may be worked out. A highly developed and active visual imagination is the greatest asset to a worker in this field, for she must not only recognise the possibly slight resemblance to a natural form, but she must be able to estimate what modifications or additional stitchery may be necessary to make it clear to others.

The second type of design is freehand and requires an outline drawing transferred to the material. It may consist of floral subjects, human figures or even landscape. The one basic essential is that the spaces to be filled by drawn fabric work should be large enough for the fillings to 'tel', and, for beginners especially, their shapes should be smooth and flowing, since jagged outlines and acute angles present difficulties which can only be surmounted by the exercise of considerable skill. The purpose for which the embroidery is to be used must always be borne in mind, and the scale of the design must be suitable both to its purpose and to the material on which the work is to be done. Templates of tinted but transparent plastic material cut into simple shapes, such as flowers, leaves or abstract forms, can be used to build up designs, for the threads of the linen being visible through them, they can be placed in the positions most convenient for the stitchery, i.e., with their greatest dimensions lying diagonally, vertically or horizontally, according to the direction of working of the proposed fillings. The rules of good design are as important in this as in other types of embroidery. If the design is poor, not even the most perfect stitchery will redeem it.

(b)   Materials

The correct foundation is linen, which may be coarse or fine, according to the size and scale of the design and the purpose for which it is intended; the finer the material, the more lacy the finished work will be. Whatever the weight of the fabric, it is important that it be fairly loosely woven, and the threads must be round and easily separated. It is impossible to work on linen which has been beaten flat or 'beetled' to give a smooth surface. Many workers prefer linen of the 'evenweave' type, that is, having an equal number of threads to the inch in warp and weft; and for geometric work, especially if the design must be a true square, this is almost essential. Most of the linens woven in this country for this type of embroidery are woven in this way, but Italian linens, which are delightful to work on, are not.

Many suitable linens are available, and amongst them the following can be confidently recommended:

For heavy work on a large scale —

Penelope Evenweave (sometimes known as Lockhart's Heavy Linen Scrim), available in white and colours,

Old Glamis 274, available in ivory, natural and colours,

For medium work —

Glenshee Evenweave, available in two widths in ivory, cream, natural and colours.

Lockhart's Finer Scrim, available in white and colours.

This is a more open fabric than Glenshee Evenweave, and is good for beginners.

Dryad's Norland Scrim, available in white and colours.

For fine work —

Lauder Gauze (fine linen scrim), available in ivory, natural and colours.

Bisso Linen, the finest scrim but not evenweave, which appears in some of the illustrations in this book, is no longer made.

For the best results a tightly twisted linen thread should be used, fine for the fillings and coarser for outlines and any padded stitches which may be introduced. D.M.C. Lin pour Dentelles, made in white and ecru, or Knox's L.C. Linen Lace Thread, in white, paris, natural, grey, whitey-brown, and also in colours in some sizes only, are the best. For fine work, sizes 50 to 70 are recommended for the fillings, 40 to 50 for medium work, 25 to 40 for heavy work; it should be finer than the threads of the material. The colour of the thread requires careful consideration. It must be remembered that the design is made by the holes which are formed by pulling apart the threads of the fabric and not by the working thread, which should therefore sink into the material. On the other hand, if the thread exactly matches the material, the work loses much of its significance and becomes flat and ineffective. It is true that the best eighteenth century work was done in white thread on white material, but the sheerness of the cambric showed up the stitchery and enhanced its value, whilst on the heavy work much rich stitchery was added to show up the delicate fillings. On the materials available to us today a thread which tones with but does not exactly match the ground gives richness to the work without distracting the eye. A contrasting colour may very occasionally be used, but only with the greatest discretion. It is not generally characteristic, and, by drawing attention away from the holes to the thread, it disturbs the balance and alters the emphasis of the work. Those wishing to use coloured linen should note that the colour range of the linen threads does not always correspond with that of the linens, and it may be found necessary to use cotton or silk threads. Pearsall's Filoselle, D.M.C. Retors Special pour Mercerie, stranded cotton or even fine crochet cotton may be tried, but they must not be expected to wear so well as the hard linen thread.

As a contrast to the open fillings, geometric satin stitch is sometimes introduced, and for this a soft thread should be used to give a smooth satiny surface. Linen floss is the best, and that made by Knox is available in a wide range of colours, but only in two sizes. It is important that the satin stitch should cover the linen without being crowded, and if linen floss of a suitable thickness is not available, then recourse must be had to a stranded thread, using the requisite number of strands to suit the linen. Pearsall's Filoselle gives satisfactory results, but if this is unobtainable, a stranded cotton will do. Both are available in a wide range of colours. Before threading the needle, each strand should be carefully separated to prevent them becoming twisted and ropey.

(c)   Other Accessories

Tapestry needles with blunt points must be used to avoid piercing the threads of the linen, and they should have eyes large enough to take the thread easily

[14]

without rubbing it. No. 24 is a useful size for fine thread, No. 22 for coarser. Pointed needles are required for finishing off threads in the fillings and for working outlines, and these too should be of a suitable size for the thread.

Some workers like to use a frame, either square or tambour, especially for working on scrim, which has a tendency to bunch up when the threads are pulled together. Those who prefer to hold the work in the hands will get equally good results by stretching the fabric firmly over the fingers. They must, however, be very careful to see that the threads of the fabric are kept quite straight; if they fall askew and are worked on in this position, it will be almost impossible to straighten the work later.

(d)   Selection of stitches

A wise selection of stitches is of prime importance, for, after the design, it is this which determines the success or failure of the whole. Fillings may be worked vertically, horizontally or diagonally; they may have an all-over effect or a definite feeling of direction; they may be heavy or light, close or lacy, rough or smooth, and all these factors must be taken into account. Select fillings which have the required effect and which at the same time are conveniently worked in the shape they are to occupy. For instance, for a long, narrow shape, if it lies along the thread, choose a filling that is worked with the thread; if it lies diagonally, use one that is worked diagonally. Aim always at contrast, which, as there is no colour, must be contrast of tone or texture. Again, the effect of any stitch is governed by the material, and a filling which is lacy on scrim may be quite heavy on linen. The use of an unfamiliar or hitherto untried fabric must therefore always be experimental, and it is prudent to have a spare piece of material on which to try the effect of stitches before using them on a design. When doing this, if the fabric is not 'evenweave', it is important to ensure that stitches which will be worked by the warp in the design are also tried out by the warp; they may look quite different if worked by the weft. Reference has already been made to the use of geometric satin stitch; another method of obtaining contrast is to leave some shapes in plain linen without stitchery, but this is only advisable when they are too small for any filling to be effective. Fairly small shapes may have fillings scaled down to suit their proportions, i.e. stitches normally worked over three threads may be worked over two. Such a scheme, however, should be carefully tested before use, lest the result be closer and heavier than was expected. Nor must crossed back stitch, commonly called 'shadow stitch', be over-

[15]

looked. It was widely used in eighteenth century work for the undulating out-lines of floral shapes, and, worked geometrically in squares, is often found in fillings alternating with open stitches.

It is a mistake to use too many fillings in a single piece of work, thus making it look fussy and restless. It is not the number of different fillings which commands attention and admiration, but the taste and discrimination shown in the suitability of each for its position in the whole. In this respect modern workers will learn much by studying good examples of old work. In some instances the apparent variety of fillings which enrich a piece are found on closer examination to be but skilful variations of a single stitch. Whether this was due to the deliberate choice of the worker or to the limitations of her knowledge it is impossible to say, but it gives the work repose and artistic unity.

The outlines in freehand work must be as carefully selected as the fillings. There is a wide variety from which to choose, ranging from the fine smoothness of whipped stem stitch to the chunkiness of double knot and the broken texture of crested chain. Each one is useful either for bringing forward a shape or strengthening a line, or for having the reverse effect, and skill and experience will guide the choice. It is important to place the emphasis in the right place, and not to give undue weight to a relatively unimportant feature. In outlining floral shapes, workers often have a definite scheme, either with fine outlines on the outer petals, working up to chunky stitchery in the heart of the flower, or vice versa.

Padded stitches are sometimes used on thick, heavy lines, but here again it is necessary to guard against over-emphasis of minor details.

Edges and borders also call for careful selection. They are the framework of the design and should be on an appropriate scale, neither so heavy as to over-weight the work nor so slight as to appear paltry. The edges generally used for linen embroidery are suitable for drawn fabric and there is a wide choice, ranging from a simple hemstitch to the picot edgings now so popular.

(e) General method of working

Beginners often ask whether it is better to work the design or to finish the edge first. This is a matter of personal choice. If the article has to be of specified dimensions, for example a tray cloth to fit a particular tray, it may be advantageous to work the edge first in order to ensure that the size is correct, and then to fit the design into it. This method is open to objection, however, since the difference of a few threads is not likely seriously to affect the over-all measure-

Plate 1. An elaborate and beautiful design symbolising the four provinces of the Union of South Africa, their sunshine, flora, wide-open spaces and history. The cloth, measuring 32 inches square, is worked on Lauder Gauze in a great variety of lacy fillings, geometric satin stitch, shadow work, bullion knots and detached bullion bars, with outlines in several kinds of chain, coral, double knot, raised chain band and buttonhole. The formal border contrasts strongly with the freehand centre and forms a well-proportioned and stabilising framework. *Worked by Mrs. van Wyk and reproduced by her permission.*

[17]

Plate 2. An example of a design composed of very few stitches. Here eyelets and raised square stitch only are used, with the edge shown in Fig. 107. Worked on Lockhart's Finer Scrim, the panel measures 11 by 8 inches.

[18]

ments, but may be quite enough to destroy the balance of the design. Experience suggests that it is usually preferable to work the design first. If this plan is adopted, the raw edges of the linen should be roughly overcast to prevent fraying, and it is helpful for the correct placing of the design to run coloured thread along the centre of the material in both directions. If the article is a large one, further threads may be run in to quarter each side, and if, in the running, the worker is careful to pick and leave a constant number of threads, usually three, much tedious counting may be saved at a later stage.

Some workers like to plan a geometric design by outlining the shapes in coloured thread, which is, of course, removed as the work progresses; others prefer to work from a plan drawn on sectional paper. Freehand designs are drawn or transferred on to the fabric, making sure that the outline is clear but not too dark, in case it is decided later to leave some spaces without a worked outline. This is occasionally done, but it demands the most careful technique.

The working thread should normally not be longer than about twelve inches; linen thread quickly rubs and gives the work a smudged woolly appearance. On the other hand, it is usually impossible to join a thread in the middle of a row, so it must be long enough to reach the end.

Fillings are always worked towards the worker, so that the pull is away from the stitchery already done. Most stitches are worked in one direction only, and at the end of each row the thread must be finished off and a fresh start made on the next row. In any shape, work the first row where the longest run can be obtained, fill half the space, then turn the work and complete the other half.

The beauty and clarity of the stitchery depends very largely on maintaining a firm, even tension. To achieve this, draw the thread through the material with a single sharp pull; a series of short tugs gives an uneven result.

The method of starting and finishing threads depends on the design and stitch in use. In normal freehand work start the thread by running it along the outline, taking a tiny back stitch to secure it, and finish it off in the same way at the end of the row. These stitches will be concealed later by the outline stitchery. In geometric designs, or in freehand work where the outline will not be worked, start by darning the needle in and out of the threads which will be covered by the first stitch, pull the thread carefully through till only the tiniest end remains, whip the threads firmly twice, and then make the first stitch. If a row of whipped stitches is to be done, the thread may be darned into the fabric where it will be gripped and hidden by the first row of stitchery. To finish off a thread, darn it into the back of the same row, and for security try to pierce the threads of the material. It may sometimes happen that a thread must be joined

[19]

in the middle of a row of open stitches, for example when working a border. In such a case the old thread is woven into the linen as invisibly as possible in a forward direction, and the new thread is run in behind the stitchery already done and brought up to the point of joining. A pointed needle is usually required for finishing off thread. When working outlines, the thread is started and finished in the same way as in other embroidery.

When fillings and outlines are completed, the work must be stretched. To do this, stitch tape along the four sides of the linen (this may be done by machine, using a long stitch), and pin it out on a board over blotting paper, setting the drawing pins through the tape as close together as is necessary to keep the linen straight and square. Then damp the linen thoroughly, cover with a cloth and leave it till quite dry. If the edges have not been worked, they should now be done and the whole thing carefully pressed, not ironed, over a very soft pad. If the edges have already been finished, the machine stitching may leave a row of tiny holes, but if the hem is gently rubbed between the fingers, these will disappear without trace.

CHAPTER III

Line stitches worked

Horizontally or vertically

This and the following chapters contain working instructions for a wide selection of stitches, with suggestions for combining them to obtain a variety of effects, and hints for their use. Some stitches are unsuitable for practical use because long loops are made on the back of the work, and these might easily catch the toe of an iron in laundering. With few exceptions, which are indicated where they occur, such stitches are not included. Stitches are referred to by the names in general use; but names have not been given to those which normally have none. Embroidery is already sufficiently bedevilled by its nomenclature without adding to the confusion. For the sake of clarity, the diagrams show only the position of the working thread, but is must be understood that each stitch is pulled very tightly to make the holes that form the pattern. Threads on the front of the work are shown as solid lines; broken lines indicate their position on the back.

Line stitches are used as frames or borders, and to connect geometric shapes; they may be spaced apart to form light or broken fillings, or they may be adapted and combined to form close fillings.

WHIPPED STITCH

This is sometimes called Pulled Satin Stitch, but the name seems misleading, since the stitch bears little resemblance to true satin stitch, but is identical with the whipped stitch used in plain sewing. That name therefore seems more appropriate. This is by far the most versatile of all drawn fabric stitches, for it may be used in a great number of ways and combines well with other stitches. It can be worked either from right to left or from left to right, horizontally or vertically, over two, three or more threads. In common usage the number is three. It is important that the stitches on the front of the work lie straight by the thread of the material, while those on the back are slanting. It consists of a row of stitches taken into every space, or into alternate spaces, as shown in Fig. 1 (a) and (b). The latter method is best worked on scrim. For the method of working this stitch diagonally, see Chapter IV.

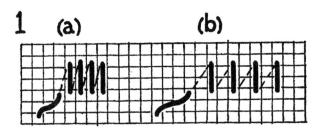

Use for lines

In normal working the thread is pulled upwards at right angles to the material, and worked thus a single row may be used as a fine line, or several rows as a border. If two rows are worked, the first with a strong pull away from the worker and the second with a strong pull towards the worker, the result is a broader line with a gap running along the centre.

Use for fillings

Successive rows of normally worked whipped stitch form a useful filling, which may, if desired, be worked to and fro across a narrow space — the only stitch with which this is possible.

If worked with the pull alternately away from and towards the worker, the result is an interesting filling with a stronger sense of direction than is given by normal working.

Basket Filling, the most popular of all open fillings, is worked entirely in this stitch. For this, start at the right, and, working towards the left, make ten stitches over three threads. Below this work a similar row back to the right, and below this a third row towards the left. Turn the work round and make a row of ten stitches at right angles to the first block. Repeat this row twice more as in the first block, then turn the work again and make a block similar to the first one. Repeat to the end of the space. The succeeding rows are worked in the same way, but

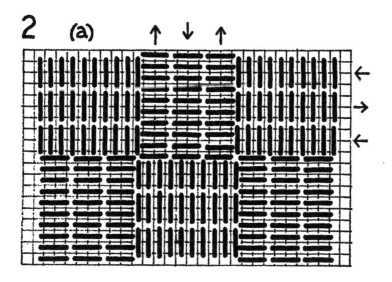

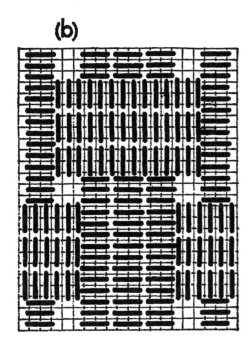

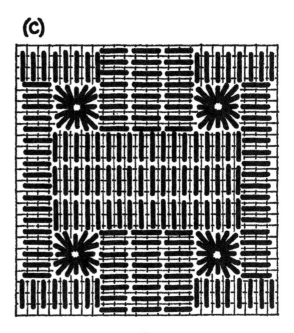

the lines of stitching in each block are at right angles to those in the one above it. (See Fig. 2 (a). The arrows show the direction of working).

As a variation of this, some threads may be left unworked at the intersections as shown in Fig. 2 (b), where squares of two threads are unworked; if larger squares are left, they may be worked as eyelets, as suggested in Fig. 2 (c). In such cases, of course, the rows of whipped stitches must be longer to cover the extra threads, and those at right angles must be accurately centred. A further variation may be obtained by making each block of two rows only, but pulled apart, leaving a gap between, as already described. These are all-over fillings, requiring plenty of room if they are to appear to advantage.

A filling with a pronounced sense of direction may be obtained by working a number of whipped stitches over six threads. Continuing in the same direction,

3

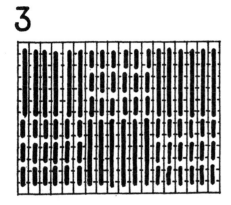

4

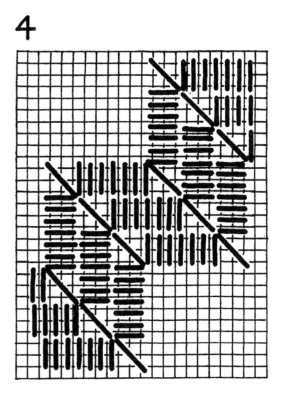

an equal number of stitches are then worked over the uppermost two threads; back over the middle two and then on again over the lowest two. The next stitches are taken over the full six threads again, and the whole operation is repeated to the end of the space. In the next row the succession is reversed, so that the narrow and wide rows alternate. See Fig. 3. This scheme is, of course, capable of infinite variation and is most effective on scrim.

If whipped stitch is worked alternately horizontally and vertically in steps, as shown in Fig. 4, a most interesting filling results. If, when changing the direction, a single diagonal stitch is made at the corner, the pull of this stitch leaves a line of holes which gives the filling a sense of direction quite opposed to that in which it is worked. This filling, also, requires plenty of room and is frequently used for corners in geometric designs. Worked on a smaller scale, for example with four stitches in each step, and without the diagonal stitch, it makes a pleasant, rather indeterminate filling.

In the filling produced by rows of normal working, the threads left exposed between the rows may themselves be whipped in groups to form a trellis or other pattern, the thread being carried carefully across the back of the original rows. This is one of the few instances where a thread of a strongly contrasting colour may be succesfully used, to emphasise the pattern of the second stage, but the filling remains effective if worked in self-colour, and is as suitable for heavy linen

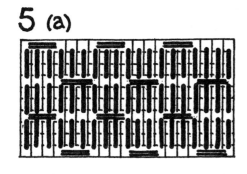

5 (a)

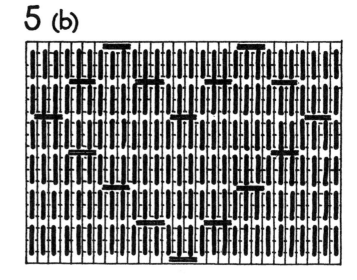

5 (b)

as for scrim. Fig. 5 (a) shows a simple trellis, (b) a heart shape, each group being whipped twice.

FLAT SQUARE STITCH

This is sometimes called Z Stitch from its appearance at the back. In front, as indicated by its name, it forms a square, and the work is quite flat. It is worked in three movements as shown in Fig. 6: —

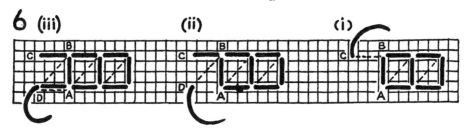

6 (iii) **(ii)** **(i)**

(1)   The needle comes up at A, goes down three threads above at B, and up three threads to the left at C.

(II)   It goes down at B, and up three threads to the left of A at D.

(III) It goes down at A and up at D again.

   This stitch is not in general use except on hems, where the stitch between B and C is omitted. Several successive rows may be worked to add weight to a hem.

RAISED SQUARE STITCH

This resembles the last stitch is being square on the front, but the back is a cross stitch with one arm doubled, and the stitch forms a pronounced ridge. It is worked either horizontally from right to left, or vertically downwards, over two, three or four threads. Used alone it forms a very distinctive line; in fillings it is usually combined with other line stitches.

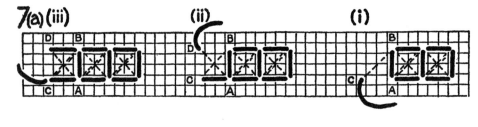
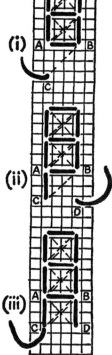

It is worked in three movements, as shown in Fig. 7.

(I)   The needle comes up at A, goes down three threads above at B, and up three threads to the left of A at C.

(II)   It goes down at A and up three threads above C at D.

(III) It goes down at B and up at C.

This stitch can be worked diagonally as shown in Chapter IV.

CHAINED BORDER STITCH

Worked from left to right, this stitch requires to be worked in a rather coarser thread. It gives a fairly heavy line with holes along the centre, and must be worked over an even number of threads, usually four or six. It is worked in two stages, each consisting of two movements, as shown in Fig. 8: —

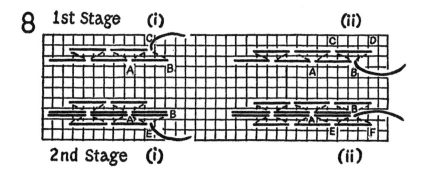

First stage —
(I)   The needle comes up at A, goes down four threads to the right at B, and up two threads to the left and one up at C.
(II) It goes down four threads to the right at D, and up again at B. These movements are repeated for the length required.
Second stage —
(I)   The needle comes up at A, goes down at B (so that the stitch from A to B is doubled), and up two threads to the left and one down at E.
(II) It goes down four threads to the right at F, and up at B.

Successive rows of this stitch, with one or two threads left between the rows, may be used as a heavy filling, but it is usually combined with other line stitches for this purpose.

BACKSTITCH

Worked from right to left, this stitch resembles ordinary backstitch, but each group of threads is bound twice and the thread is caught into the material on alternate sides so that the stitches lie smoothly side by side. This is an invaluable stitch for a fine but well-defined line. Fig. 9 shows the method of working: —
(I)   The needle comes up at A, goes down three threads to the right at B, and up again at A.

(II)   It goes down at B, and up one thread below A at C.

(III) It goes down at A, up three threads to the left at D, down at A and up at D again, then down at A and up one thread above D at E.

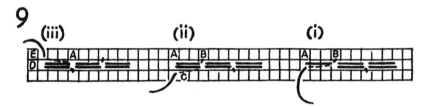

For a light, open filling, this stitch may be used, spaced apart at suitable intervals; it also combines well with other stitches, and may be worked diagonally as shown in Chapter IV.

BACKSTITCH VARIATION

This is well-known as a filling, though it appears to have no generally recognised name, but it also forms a useful line, when a broader and more definite effect is desired. It is worked from right to left in four movements as shown in Fig. 10: —

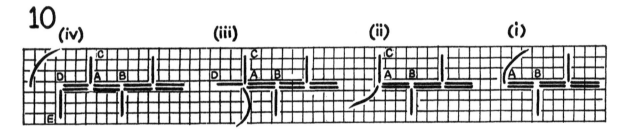

(I)   The needle comes up at A, goes down three threads to the right at B, and up at A. This movement is repeated once.

(II)   It goes down three threads above A at C, and up at A.

(III) It goes down three threads to the left of A at D, and up at A. (This is an awkward movement).

(IV)   It goes down at D, up three threads below D at E, down again at D, and up three threads to the left, ready to start with the first movement again.

The filling consists of successive rows, worked so that the protruding stitches meet, and it has a light square effect with a slight sense of direction.

THREE-SIDED STITCH

This consists of a row of triangles with the points facing alternately up and down. It makes a very heavy line with well-defined holes. It is worked from right to left over an even number of threads, and the method is shown in Fig. 11: —

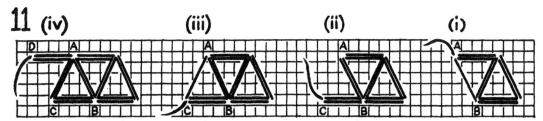

(I)   The needle comes up at A, goes down four threads down and two to the right at B, and up at A.

(II) It goes down at B, and up four threads to the left at C. This movement is repeated twice more.

(III) It goes down at A, and up at C.

(IV) It goes down at A, and up four threads to the left at D. This movement is repeated twice more.

Successive rows of this stitch, usually with one or two threads of the linen left between each row, is used for a very heavy filling with a strong sense of direction. The method of working this stitch diagonally is described in Chapter IV, and suggestions for adapting it to form isolated units will be found in Chapter VII.

RINGED BACKSTITCH

This is a very broad and decorative line stitch which is often used for borders. The 'rings' are really eight-sided figures, each side consisting of two back stitches worked over two threads. It is worked from right to left in two stages, the first forming the upper part of the rings, which are completed in the second stage. There are several methods of working; that shown in Fig. 12 is considered to be the simplest: —

First stage —

(I)   The needle comes up at A, goes down two threads below at B, up at A, down at B, and up two threads to the left and two higher than A at C.

(II) It goes down at A, up at C, down at A, and up two threads to the left of C at D.

(III) It goes down at C, up at D, down at C, and up two threads to the left and two lower than D at E.

(IV) It goes down at D, up at E, down at D, and up two threads below E at F.

(V) It goes down at E, up at F, down at E, and up two threads to the left and two higher than E at G.

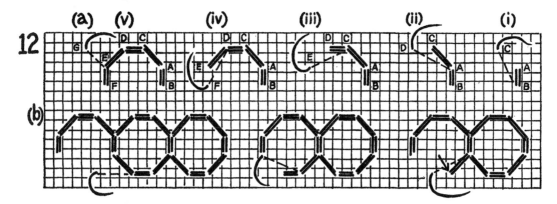

This movement commences the second ring, and this stage is repeated from (II) to the end of the row. The lower sides of the rings are worked in exactly the same way. The arrow in Fig. 12 (b) shows the starting point of this second stage. This stitch may be worked diagonally as shown in Chapter IV, and its use as a filling is described in Chapter V.

WAVED BACKSTITCH

This is on the same scale as Ringed Backstitch and is used in the same way. It is a wavy line of backstitches, worked from right to left over two threads, in

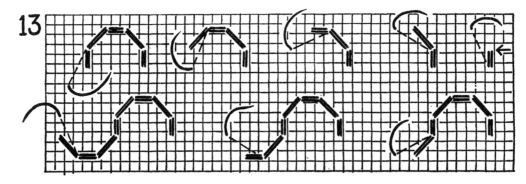

exactly the same way as Ringed Backstitch. The method is so straightforward that detailed instructions are superfluous. Fig. 13 shows the direction of the stitches, starting from the arrow. A light filling is formed by working rows of this stitch with no intervening threads, so that the top stitch of one row is on the same level as the bottom stitch of the preceding one.

COMBINING STITCHES TO FORM FILLINGS

These, then, are the basic line stitches worked horizontally and vertically. They may, as already stated, be used as lines, and in some cases they may form fillings, but they may also be mixed together to make fillings. The possibilities are endless, but it should be noted that all such fillings are more or less heavy in character, and that they have a very strong sense of direction. They are, therefore, particularly suitable for longshapes, either to emphasise the length and direction, or to give a striped effect in contrast with other neigbouring fillings.

Several repeats are necessary before the full effect of the filling is seen. Where whipped stitch is combined with others, it will be found easier in practice to work all the whipped stitches first, for once threads are pulled together in another stitch, it is difficult to introduce the needle between them again. The most succesful combinations are made up of stitches which contrast with each other, and some which have proved satisfactory are listed below.

(1)   One row of Whipped Stitch, pulled downwards.
        One row of Three-sided Stitch.
        One row of Whipped Stitch, pulled upwards.
This gives heavy stripes with large holes and a gap between the stripes.

(2)   One row of Whipped Stitch, pulled downwards.
        One row of Raised Square Stitch.
        One row of Whipped Stitch, pulled upwards.
This gives medium stripes with a gap between them, and is particularly attractive on scrim.

(3)   One row of Whipped Stitch, pulled downwards.
        One row of Chained Border Stitch.
        One row of Whipped Stitch, pulled upwards.
These are heavy stripes with the thicker thread of the Chained Border Stitch giving a rich effect, and a gap between them.

(4)   One row of Whipped Stitch, pulled downwards.

[31]

Leave one thread of the linen.
One row of Backstitch.
Leave one thread of the linen.
One row of Whipped Stitch, pulled upwards.
These are narrower stripes marked by the holes of the Backstitch, and with a gap between them.

(5)   One row of Whipped Stitch, pulled downwards.
One row of Waved Backstitch.
One row of Whipped Stitch, pulled upwards.
These are broader, lighter stripes with a gap between them.

(6)   Three rows of Whipped Stitch and one row of Raised Square Stitch, with one thread of linen left between each row.
The numbers of rows of each stitch can be varied, but it is better to let one stitch predominate.

(7)   Like (6), but worked horizontally and vertically in steps of five squares. In this case the Raised Square Stitch should be worked first.

(8)   Alternate rows of Whipped Stitch and Backstitch Variation, with one thread left between each row.
This gives a fairly light filling, with the holes of the Backstitch showing up strongly.

(9)   Alternate rows of Three-sided Stitch and Ringed Backstitch, with one thread left between each row.
This is a rich filling, with the heavy narrow rows contrasting with the lighter and wider ones.

(10)   Alternate rows of Chained Border Stitch and Backstitch worked over two threads, with one thread left between each row.
This is a rich, close filling, relieved by the holes made by both the component stitches.

(11)   Alternate rows of Whipped Stitch and Ringed Backstitch, with three threads left between each row.
This is a rather light, open filling, which requires a lot of space to be effective

(12)   Alternate rows of Flat Square Stitch and Backstitch, with one thread left between each row.
This is a fairly light, rather indeterminate filling, suitable, where not much emphasis is required.

This list could be extended almost indefinitely, but it is already long enough to indicate some of the arrangements which can be devised, and the variety of effects which can be obtained.

CHAPTER IV

Line stitches

Worked diagonally

Many of the line stitches described in Chapter III may also, with slight modifications, be worked diagonally, and this is particularly useful when they are used as borders or frames, as the diagonal form may be worked across the corners to soften the rigidity of a rectangle. The change of direction sometimes presents a problem, but experience and imagination will suggest means of overcoming it.

These stitches are used for the same purposes as those worked horizontally and vertically, and, like them, can be mixed in various ways as fillings. In addition, however, some of them may be worked in successive rows, and the fillings thus formed are amongst the most widely used of all drawn fabric fillings. Working on the diagonal is a little more difficult than working by the thread, for the diagonal pull tends to distort the material and makes it difficult to see where the needle should go.

It is necessary to be particularly careful in working the first row of a filling, because any inaccuracy will probably not be detected till the next row is being worked, and both rows must then be unpicked — a weary process which it is worth taking much trouble to avoid.

DIAGONAL WHIPPED STITCH

This is worked in exactly the same way as when worked by the thread, but the surface stitches lie on the diagonal as shown in Fig. 14 (a) and (b). It can be worked sloping upwards or downwards, and either from right to left or from left to right. As a single line it is less distinct than the straight form and it shows up best on scrim, but successive rows worked one thread apart, as shown in Fig.

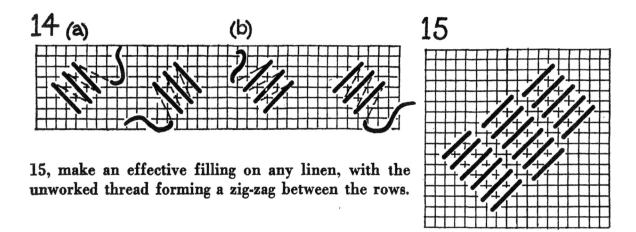

14 (a) (b) **15**

15, make an effective filling on any linen, with the unworked thread forming a zig-zag between the rows.

DIAGONAL RAISED SQUARE STITCH

This may be worked downwards or upwards, but always from right to left. It is worked downwards in the same way as the horizontal form, the only difference being in passing from one square to the next, as shown in Fig. 16 (a): —

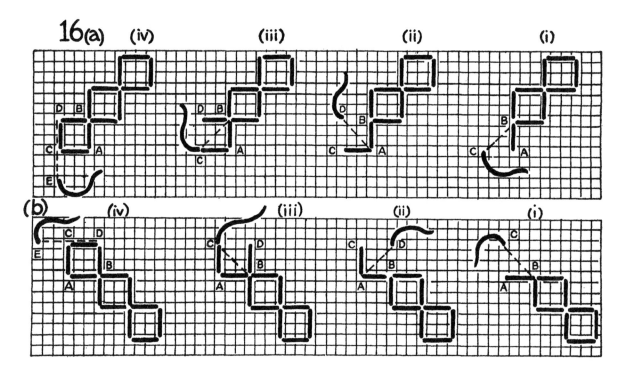

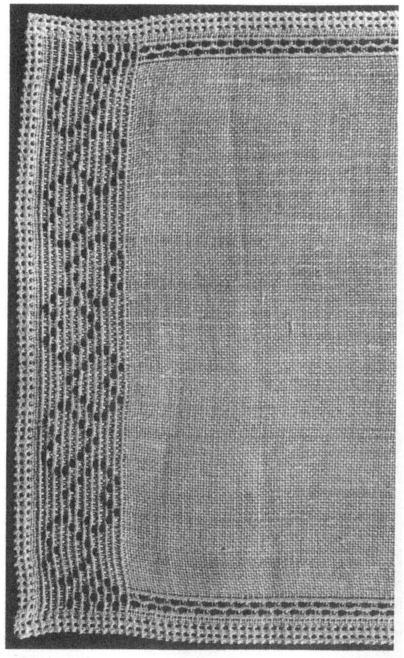

Plate 3 Rows of whipped stitch have the exposed threads whipped in a contrasting colour as in Fig. 5 (b). The material is pink Penelope Evenweave, with the hearts in dark red. Fig. 106 shows the edge.

Plate 4 Eyelets and raised square stitch suggest a conventional flower spray. This detail, measuring 7½ by 1½ inches, is worked on Lauder Gauze.

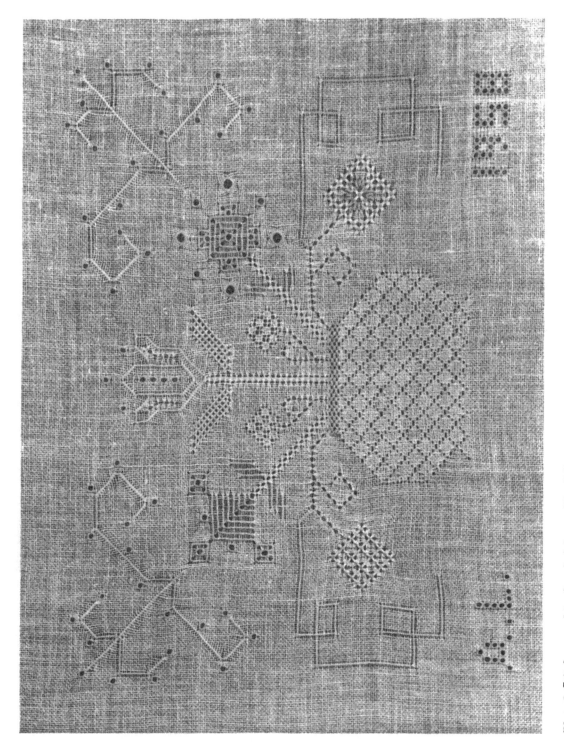

Plate 5 Stitches combined and elaborated in different ways suggest flower shapes. Worked on *Lauder Gauze*, the panel measures 12 by 9 inches and the stitches include eyelets, open trellis, Greek cross, detached whipped bars and several line stitches. Fig. 37 (b).

17

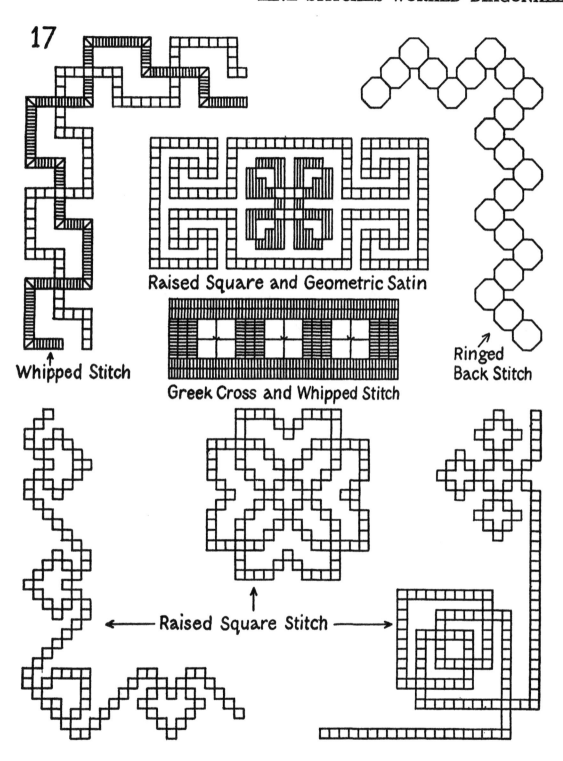

Raised Square and Geometric Satin

Greek Cross and Whipped Stitch

Whipped Stitch

Ringed
Back Stitch

← Raised Square Stitch →

(I)   The needle comes up at A, goes down three threads above at B, and up three threads to the left of A at C.

(II)   It goes down at A, and up three threads above C at D.

(III) It goes down at B, and up at C.

(IV)   It goes down at D, and up three threads below C at E. This movement leaves a long thread on the back, but in the next stitch the needle should pass down to the right of this thread and so catch it up and draw it out of sight.

Working upwards is a little more awkward, and many workers find it easier to turn the work so that they are still working downwards. The upwards method is shown in Fig. 16 (b) : —

(I)   The needle comes up at A, goes down three threads to the right at B, and up three threads above A at C.

(II)   It goes down at A, and up three threads above B at D.

(III) It goes down at B, and up at C.

(IV)   It goes down at D, and up three threads to the left of C at E.

This again leaves a long thread on the back, but if it is caught up by the next stitch in the way already described, the work will be perfectly neat.

Both the straight and diagonal forms of this stitch can be used, either separately, or together, to build up interesting geometric designs, and those based on the Greek key pattern or on Celtic knots are very effective. Some simple suggestions on these lines will be found in Fig. 17.

DIAGONAL CHAINED BORDER

Worked upwards from left to right, the movements correspond exactly with those of the form worked horizontally or vertically. Fig. 18 shows the position

18

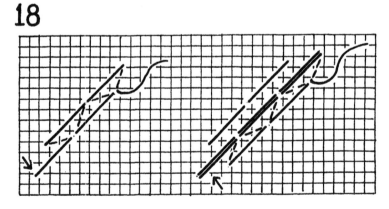

of the thread in the two stages, with the arrow indicating the starting point, and no further explanation is required.

DIAGONAL BACKSTITCH

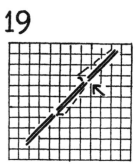

19

This again has the same method of working as that worked horizontally or vertically, but the holes appear larger and the effect is more definite. It is worked downwards from right to left, and Fig. 19 shows the position of the stitches.

DIAGONAL THREE-SIDED STITCH

Although the method of working is exactly the same, in order to preserve the scale the diagonal form is worked over fewer threads, as Fig. 20 (a) clearly shows.

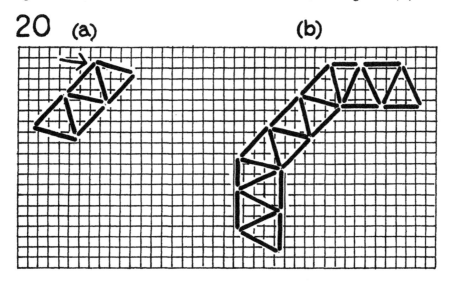

20 (a) (b)

Any change of direction calls for some adjustment, and Fig. 20 (b) suggests how this can be arranged. Once the straightforward method has been mastered, these adjustments will present no difficulty.

[39]

DIAGONAL RINGED BACKSTITCH

The 'rings' are connected on a diagonal side instead of on a straight one. The stitch is worked downwards from right to left; the method remains the same and

21

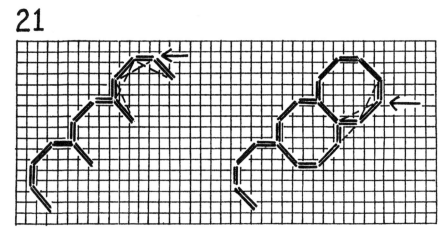

any change of direction is carried out without difficulty. See Fig. 21. An attractive border shown in Fig. 17 will doubtless inspire other ideas and variations.

DIAGONAL WAVED BACKSTITCH

Again the method remains the same and the stitch is worked downwards from right to left as shown in Fig. 22.

22

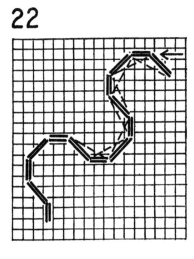

The stitches which follow are diagonal stitches in their own right, that is to say that they do not exactly correspond with any stitch worked horizontally or vertically. They may be used, in single or double rows, for lines; successive rows may be worked as fillings, or single rows spaced at suitable intervals form useful light fillings which may be varied according to taste and requirements.

SINGLE FAGGOT

This is the simplest of all the diagonal stitches. It is worked downwards from right to left, over two, three or four threads, and has straight stitches forming steps on the front, with diagonal stitches on the back. The two movements are shown in Fig. 23: —

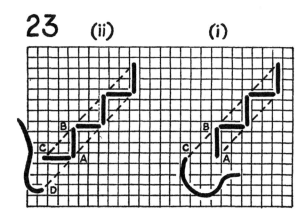

(I)   The needle comes up at A, goes down three threads above at B, and up three threads to the left of A at C.

(II) It goes down at A, and up three threads below C at D.

A single row of this is rarely used, but a double row arranged so that the steps form squares, makes a good line, though the double working is tedious, and it has been largely superseded by Diagonal Raised Square Stitch.

Successive rows make a light filling with an all-over effect, and by leaving one

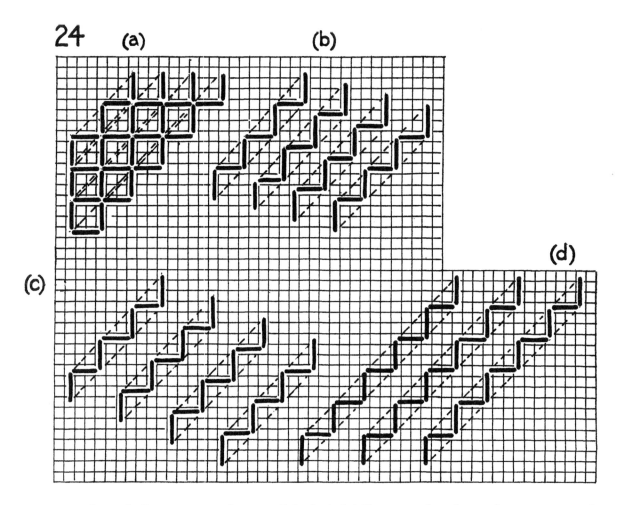

or more threads between each row delightful fillings with a lacy character result. See Fig. 24.

DOUBLE FAGGOT

This is worked in the same way as Single Faggot, but each stitch is doubled and it is usually worked over two threads. Fig. 25 shows the method: —

(I)   The needle comes up at A, goes down two threads above at B, up at A, down at B, and up two threads to the left of A at C.

(II) It goes down at A, up at C, down at A, and up two threads below C at D. This makes a much more definite line than Single Faggot, and rows of it worked several threads apart form a light striped filling. A variation of it with which several different fillings can be built up is described in Chapter VI.

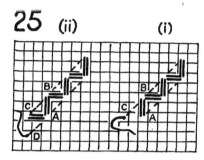

REVERSED FAGGOT

This is sometimes known as 'Yee', but the usual name describes it well, for it is the exact reverse of Single Faggot. It is worked upwards from left to right and

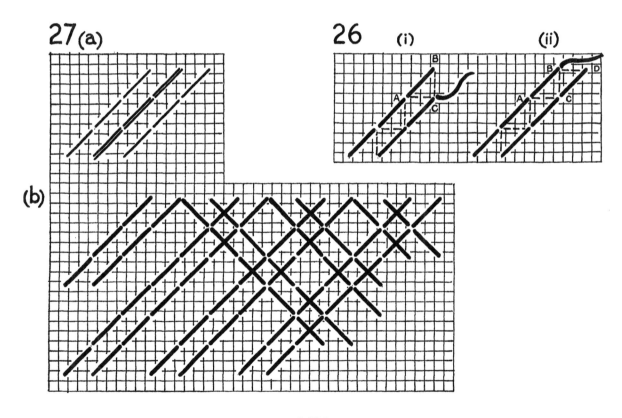

shows diagonal stitches on the front with straight stitches on the back. Fig. 26 shows the method: —

(I)   The needle comes up at A, goes down three threads to the right and three higher at B, and up three threads to the right of A at C.

(II) It goes down three threads to the right of B at D, and up at B.

A double row of this worked as indicated in Fig. 27 (a) produces a heavy line which is often used to outline geometric shapes.

Successive rows form a heavy, close filling with a fairly strong sense of direction. Single rows spaced six threads apart give a light striped effect and if, in addition, similar rows running in the opposite direction are added, the result is a light trellis. See Fig. 27 (b).

WHIPPED REVERSE FAGGOT

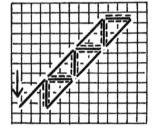

28

By repeating each movement once more, a straight stitch is added to the diagonal ones, giving a more definite effect. Fig. 28 shows the position of the thread. A single row of this makes a good line, and may be used in the same way as double faggot.

GREEK CROSS

This is a delightful and most adaptable stitch, each cross consisting of four blanket stitches with the heads together and the legs radiating to the four points of the compass. Hence it is sometimes called 'North-East-South-West'. The crosses are usually worked diagonally, either upwards or downwards, and either from right to left or vice versa. Working downwards from right to left seems to give the clearest result, and this method is shown in Fig. 29. Once workers understand this method and see clearly what the result should be, they can try other methods and use that which is preferred.

(I)   The needle comes up at A, goes down three threads to the right and three higher at B, and up three threads to the right of A at C, making a blanket stitch.

[44]

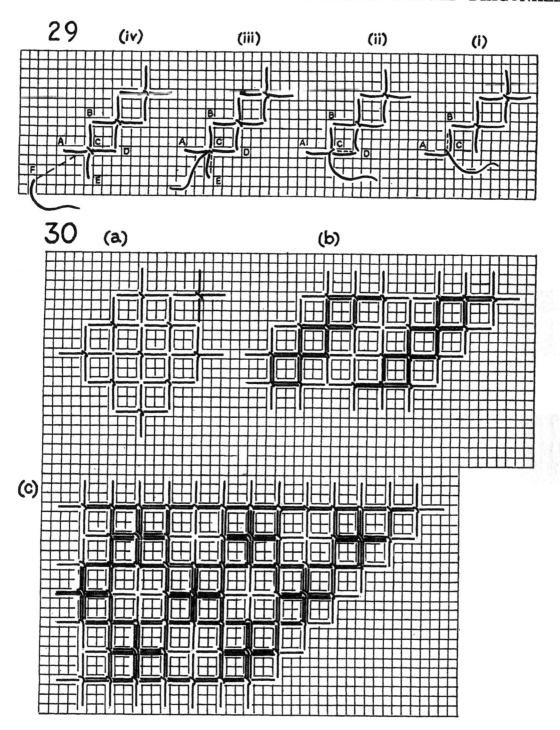

31   (a)

(b)

(c)

(d)

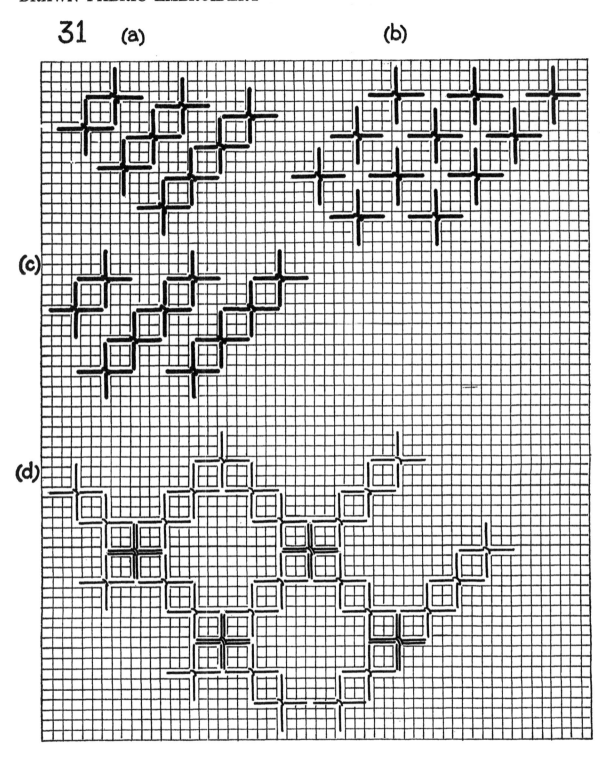

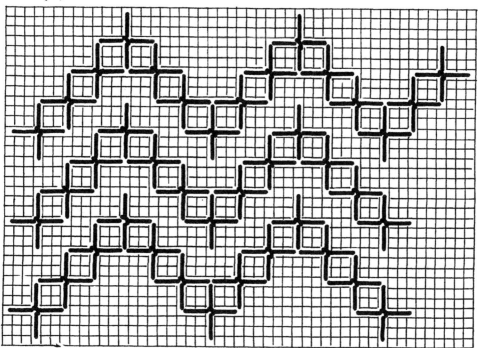

(II)   It goes down three threads to the right of C at D, and up at C, again making a blanket stitch.

(III)   It goes down three threads below C at E, and up at C, again making a blanket stitch.

(IV)   It goes down at C, but inside the loop formed by the first movement, and comes up six threads to the left of E at F, where it is in position to start the next cross.

A single row of this stitch gives a rather broad line with large holes on both sides; successive rows give a very definite all-over filling, with large holes where the arms of the crosses meet. Over this filling further rows, spaced at intervals, may be worked, making the crosses interlace, so that the centres of the new crosses fill the holes previously made. This gives a diagonal stripe, but if again further rows are spaced lying across the last ones, a rich, heavy trellis effect is obtained. See Fig. 30.

More open fillings result from spacing rows or stitches one or more threads apart, or spaced rows may be arranged to form an open trellis. Again, by working a constant number of stitches alternately upwards and downwards. chevron lines are made, which, when spaced apart, form a filling with a strong sense of direction. Fig. 31 illustrates these ideas.

Worked on a larger scale, for instance over six threads instead of three, this stitch can be used as a repeating unit in a border, alternating with blocks of some other stitch. In Fig. 17 Whipped Stitch is suggested for this purpose, but blocks of Satin Stitch would be equally suitable.

INDIAN DRAWN GROUND

This charming stitch is believed to have been found on Indian eighteenth century work, but was not, so far as is known, used in European work. Its delicacy makes it suitable only for fine open scrim, particularly where a dark mount, as in cushions or tea cosies, or where light shining through, as in curtains and lampshades, shows it up to perfection. It consists of a series of squares, joined diagonally, and generally two rows, to form chevrons, are worked back to back, with the thread travelling round each square, clockwise in one row and anti-clockwise in the other. Fig. 32 shows the method: —

First row —

(I) The needle comes up at A, goes down three threads to the left at B, up three threads higher at C, down three to the right at D, and up at A again.

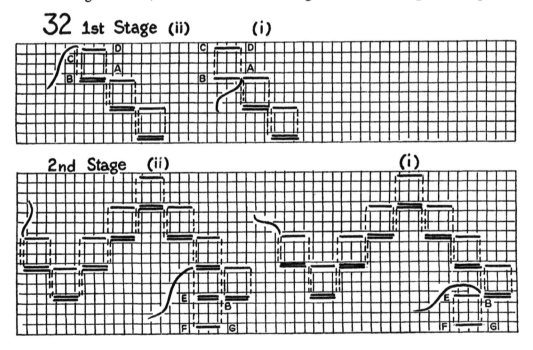

32 1st Stage (ii)   (i)

2nd Stage (ii)   (i)

(II) It goes down at B, up at C, and from there starts the next square. These movements are repeated for the required length.

Second row —

(1) The needle comes up at B, goes down three threads to the left at E, up three threads lower at F, down three threads to the right at G, and up at B again.

(II) It goes down at E, up three threads higher at the corner of a square of the first row, and from there starts the next square.

COMBINING STITCHES TO FORM FILLINGS

Filling formed by mixing two of these stitches can be very effective, given plenty of room. They are not suitable for small spaces, and are mostly heavy with a strong sense of direction. Here are some ideas for such mixtures: —

(I) Alternate rows of Diagonal Whipped Stitch and Diagonal Ringed Backstitch with one thread left between each row.

(II) Alternate rows of Diagonal Whipped Stitch and Diagonal Waved Backstitch with one thread left between each row.

(III) A double row of Reversed Faggot.
Leave six threads.
One row of Diagonal Backstitch.
Leave six threads.

(IV) Two rows of Diagonal Raised Square Stitch with one thread left between the rows.
Leave three threads.
A double row of Reversed Faggot.
Leave three threads.

(V) Alternate rows of Diagonal Whipped Stitch and Double Faggot with three threads left between the rows.

(VI) Three rows of Diagonal Whipped Stitch with one thread left between the rows.
Leave two threads.
A double row of Reversed Faggot.
Leave two threads.

(VII) Groups of three successive rows of Reversed Faggot with six threads left between the groups.

[49]

(VIII) Alternate rows of Single Faggot and Reversed Faggot.
As one is worked downwards and the other upwards, these rows can be worked continuously as long as the thread lasts.

(IX) One row of Single Faggot.
One row of Reversed Faggot.
One row of Single Faggot.
These three rows make up a unit which is repeated at intervals to give a striped effect.

(X) Two rows of Greek Cross alternating with three rows of Reversed Faggot.

(XI) Alternate rows of Greek Cross worked over five threads and Whipped Stitch worked in steps.

(XII) Two rows of Single Faggot worked one thread apart alternating with one row of Whipped Stitch worked in steps.

In the last two suggestions the placing of the stitches is difficult to describe in words, but diagrams will be found in Fig. 33 (a) and (b). It must be stressed that these diagrams merely show the position of the stitches; they give no

33 (a)

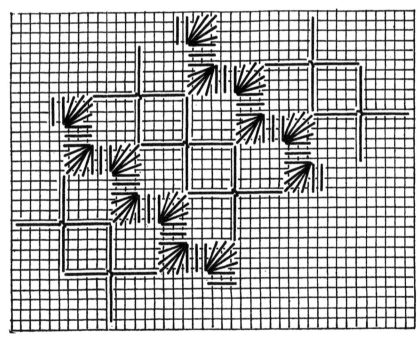

(b)

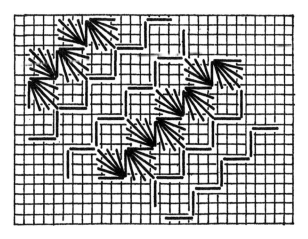

idea of the striking contrast between the open stripes of Greek Cross or Single Faggot and the close lines of Whipped Stitch. To get the best effect these two fillings should be worked on scrim.

CHAPTER V

Fillings worked

Horizontally and vertically

The fillings form the principal characteristic of drawn fabric embroidery, and it is on the careful selection, placing and working of them that the beauty and success of the work chiefly depends. They have an unending fascination for workers, who devote much time to learning and practising them, and, with increasing experience and confidence, devising new variations, each according to her fancy. There is a strong temptation to use a large number of fillings in a single article; but this temptation should be firmly resisted by the exercise of strict self-discipline. However elaborate a piece of work may be, it will be more coherent and satisfying if the number of fillings be rigidly controlled, though a number of variations of one filling may be introduced with great success. As an example of this, a very lovely eighteenth century frill may be mentioned. It has a floral border which at first sight appears to contain many different fillings, giving a rich variety of effects. When these fillings were examined and analysed, however, it was found that most of them were variations of Reversed Wave Stitch, some of which appear in Fig. 42.

It may be helpful at this point to explain the system of classification of fillings which has been adopted in this and the next chapter. Fillings have in the past been grouped in a variety of ways, not always very helpful to the worker seeking a filling for a particular purpose. The choice is in the last analysis governed by two factors, viz., the direction of working and the effect of the filling when completed, and it was felt that to classify fillings on these broad principles would be the most practical method to employ here. Some overlapping is inevitable, but in the main this chapter describes fillings worked horizontally or vertically, in the first section those with an all-over effect, and in the second those with a sence of direction. Chapter VI deals with fillings worked on the diagonal and grouped according to the same plan.

Instructions for most of the stitches used have already been given in Chapters III and IV, and some simple fillings built up on them, without any modifications, have already been described. The fillings which follow show how they may be modified and adapted, and demonstrate that the variations of effect depend on the proportions of each stitch, and on the position in relation to each other of both stitches and rows of stitches.

(a)   FILLINGS WITH AN ALL-OVER EFFECT

The simplest of all fillings consists of Running Stitch, picking up three threads and leaving three threads and placing the stitches alternately up and down by

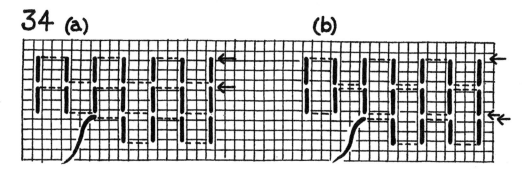

three threads. The two alternative forms are shown in Fig. 34 (a) and (b), the latter being more clearly defined. This is a filling to use where little emphasis is required.

Ringed Backstitch makes a fairly large-scale and well defined filling of great

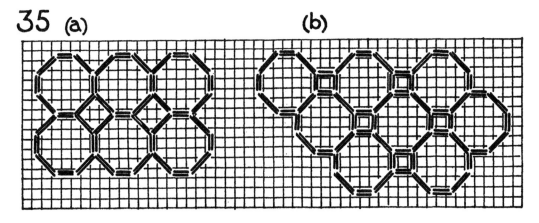

[53]

charm, suitable for any weight of linen. There are two forms as shown in Fig. 35 (a) and (b), and it is worked in the same way as the line stitch, half rings being worked in each row. A variation shown in Fig. 36 is on a larger scale and is worked differently. Each row consists of two Raised Square Stitches,

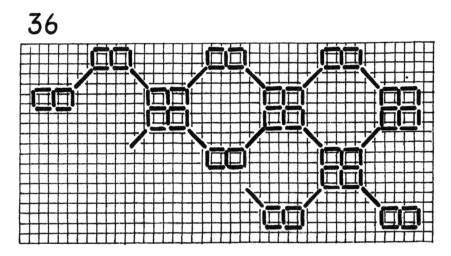

36

followed by a Diagonal Backstitch travelling alternately upwards and downwards. In the second and subsequent rows the Raised Square Stitches have three sides only, as the top side has been supplied by the previous row.

Two lacy fillings are based on Diagonal Backstitch taken over two threads. The first, shown in Fig. 37 (a), gives the effect of squares separated by double crosses and is worked thus. Starting at the arrow, two Backstitches are made over a diagonal of two threads, the needle is carried horizontally to the left under

37 (a)   (b)

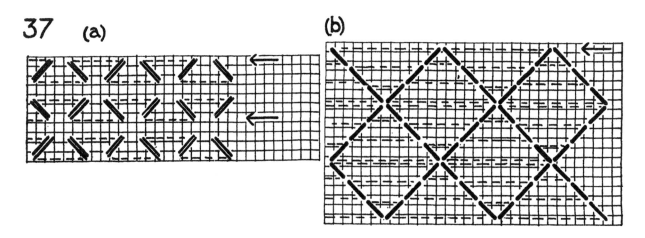

six threads and two more Backstitches are made but on the opposite diagonal. The needle is carried again under six threads, and these movements are repeated to the end of the row. Two threads are left between each row, and the position of the Backstitches in the succeeding rows is shown in the diagram. The second filling, shown in Fig. 37 (b), makes an open trellis, which is particularly charming on scrim. It should be noted, however, that the long threads lying on the back make it only suitable for work that is to be framed. The diagram shows only single Backstitches, but on any other material than fine open scrim each stitch should be doubled to give more definition. Starting at the arrow, the needle goes down two threads to the right and two down, and passes horizontally to the left under four threads. It goes down at the starting point and passes horizontally under twelve threads, and these two movements are repeated to the end of the row. The next row starts at the foot of the first Backstitch, and the movements are identical but the needle passes under eight threads in both movements. In the third row it passes under twelve threads and then under four. These three rows are then repeated in reverse order, with the Backstitches lying on the opposite diagonal to form a lattice.

Honeycomb, a well-tried and ever-popular filling, has a rough texture owing to the thread lying on the surface, and is suitable for all materials. It is worked vertically downwards in two movements, as shown in Fig. 38: —

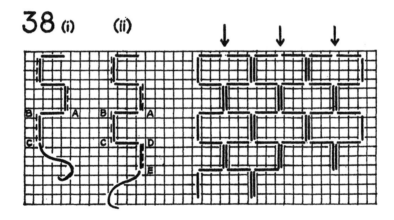

(I)   The needle comes up at A, down three threads to the left at B, up three threads down at C, down at B and up at C.

(II) It goes down three threads below A at D, up three threads lower at E, down at D, and up at E.

In the next row, starting at the same point, the first movement is made to the right instead of to the left. Thus all the vertical stitches are doubled. The filling consists of these two rows repeated till the area is covered, and the third row is started six threads to the right of the starting point of the first and second rows.

Wave Stitch makes a simple, straight forward filling with a somewhat indeterminate appearance. It is worked horizontally from right to left in two movements as shown in Fig. 39 (a): —

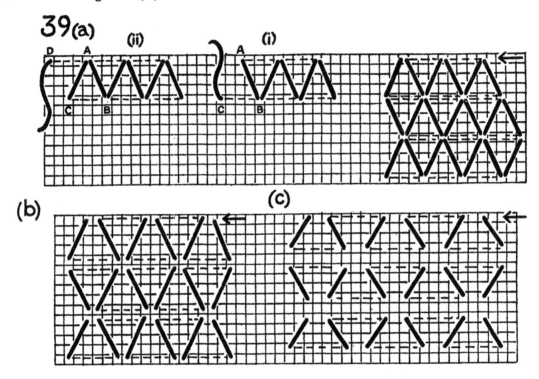

(I)   The needle comes up at A, goes down two threads to the right and four down at B, up four threads to the left at C.

(II) It goes down at A, and up four threads to the left at D.

The rows are worked successively with no intervening threads. If, however, one thread is left between each stitch and each row, as in Fig. 39 (b), it is called Window Filling, and if two threads are left, as in Fig. 39 (c), it is known as Double Window Filling. Both Window and Double Window Fillings are more defined than Wave Stitch Filling.

An attractive variation, found in eighteenth century work, consists of Wave Stitch Filling worked on a larger scale as shown in Fig. 40. Over this diagonal lines are worked to form a trellis, in which one thread above and one thread below a hole are caught together in a single Backstitch.

40

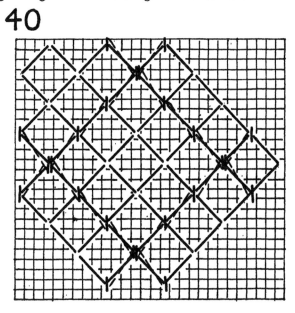

41 (a)

→

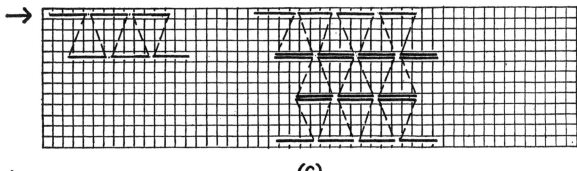

(b)   (c)

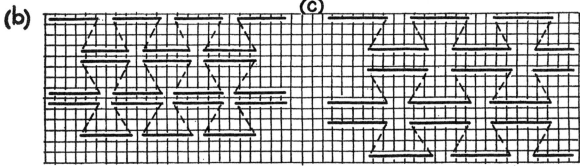

In Wave Stitch the surface stitches are diagonal, those on the back horizontal. If these are reversed and worked from left to right, as in Fig. 41 (a), a rather heavier filling results, and again stitches and rows may be worked one thread or two threads apart, as in Fig. 41 (b) and (c). This Reversed Wave Stitch can be varied by altering the number of threads in each stitch, doubling the stitch if necessary to give clearer definition and by stepping the stitches upwards and downwards to form a broken trellis. Fig. 42 shows four such arrangements. They are particularly attractive on fine scrim, and some require plenty of room to be fully effective. Eyelets or blocks of Satin Stitch may be set in the spaces if liked.

Again the same stitch, worked in horizontal rows spaced apart, and crossed by rows similarly spaced, gives a pleasing lacy filling with a squared effect, but without the monotony which sometimes attends squared fillings. Fig. 43 shows the position of the rows in relation to each other.

Rows of Whipped Stitch, with the stitches spaced apart, and crossed by similar

43

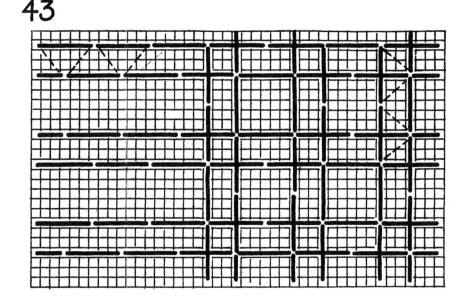

rows, give the well-known Cobbler and Framed Cross Fillings. Cobbler Fillings, shown in Fig. 44 (a), has the stitches alternately four threads and two threads apart, and two threads divide the rows. In Framed Cross Filling, shown in Fig. 44 (b), the stitches are four threads and one thread apart, and one thread separates the rows. These fillings are both very clearly defined and suitable for all materials.

42

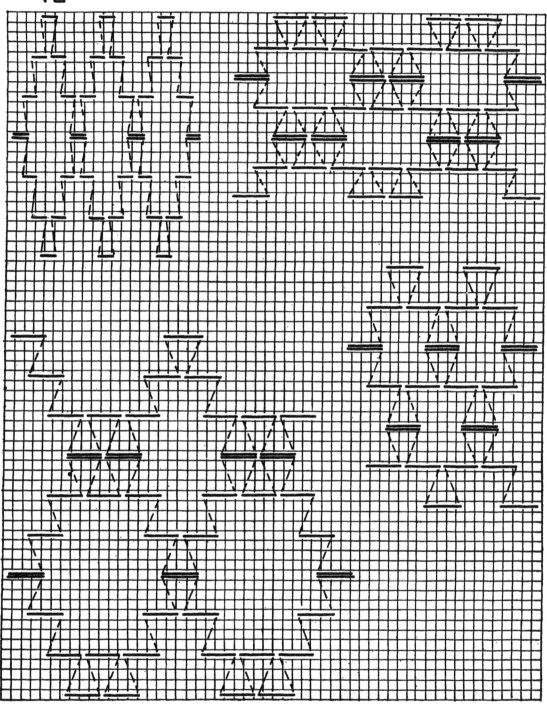

44

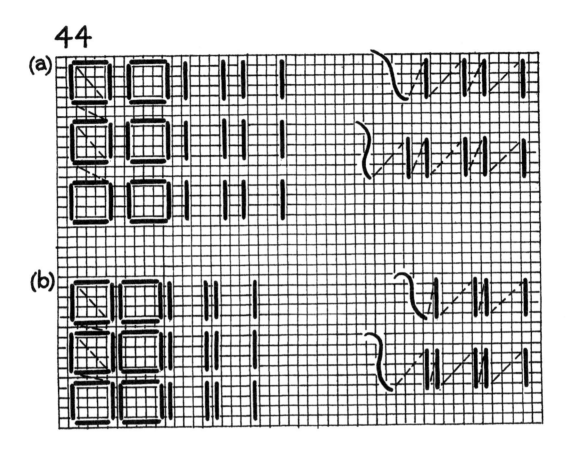

Many other spacings of stitches and rows can be tried; an arrangement like that in Fig. 45, where whipped stitches are worked in groups, either in rows or steps, leaves blank squares which may then be enriched with further stitchery worked on the diagonal. Three suggestions for this diagonal stitchery are shown. In the first one, Fig. 45 (a), the needle comes up at the top right hand-corner of the square. It goes down again in the same hole and comes up in the lower left-hand corner with the thread looped round it to form a Chain Stitch. It then goes down again in the same hole, and, passing diagonally under the intersection of the whipped rows, comes up in the top right-hand corner of the next square on the diagonal. The second method, in Fig. 45 (b), is worked upwards by picking up each square and intersection with a Backstitch as though working Stem Stitch. At the end of the row the needle is passed to the back and comes up in the first hole of the line already worked on one side of the thread forming the Stem Stitch. It goes dwn on the other side of this thread, thus catching it down, and comes up at the next hole, and in this way it travels back to the beginning of the row. If either of these methods is used on every diagonal and is then crossed by similar lines on the opposite diagonal, the result is a very rich, close filling. The third method of obtaining a somewhat similar effect is to work

45

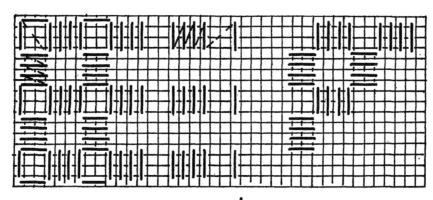

(a)

(b)

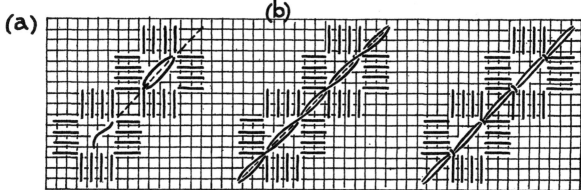

(c)

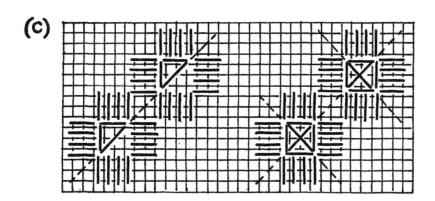

a Framed Cross in each square. This is best done in two journeys, as shown in Fig. 45 (c). Working downwards on the diagonal, the thread is fastened behind the first intersection and is brought op at the lower left-hand corner of the square. It goes down at the top left-hand corner and up at the top right-hand corner, down again at the top left-hand corner and up at the lower left-hand corner, which completes half the frame. To make half the cross the needle then goes down at the top right-hand corner, and, passing under the intersection, comes up at the lower left-hand corner of the next square on the diagonal, where the process is repeated. When the whole surface has been thus covered, the opposite diagonals are worked in the same way, completing the frame and the cross. As

46

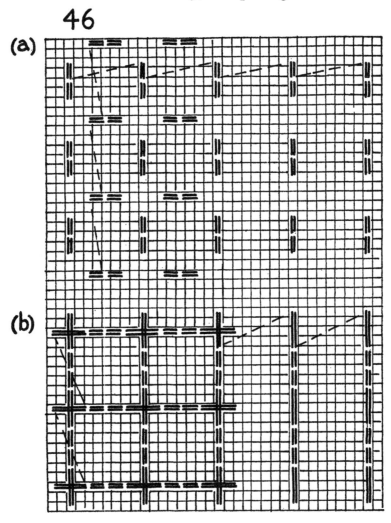

before, the effect is rich and heavy, and if held against the light the framed crosses with the long oblique threads lying at the back look like little stars.

An even closer, richer effect can be obtained by working the Stem Stitch diagonals already described over a filling of Double Faggot.

A delightful but unobtrusive filling on a fairly large scale is very simply made by working a row of double Whipped Stitches over two threads, leaving eight threads between the stitches. Close under this a similar row is worked, then four threads are left and two more are worked. When the space is covered, similar rows are worked across. The position of the rows in relation to each other is shown in Fig. 46 (a). A more definite and elaborate version of this filling is made by adding double Whipped Stitches over the intervening four threads, as shown in Fig. 46 (b). The crossing of these longer stitches adds emphasis and character to the filling.

Punch Stitch is also composed of successive rows of double Whipped Stitches worked over four threads and spaced four threads apart. Similar rows are then worked across, and the whole filling forms an open squared ground, very suitable for medium or heavy linen. See Fig. 47.

Diagonal Whipped Stitch worked in horizontal zig-zag rows covers the ground with a diamond lattice, and with eyelets worked in each diamond forms a delightful and very positive filling, suitable for most materials. It is shown in Fig. 48.

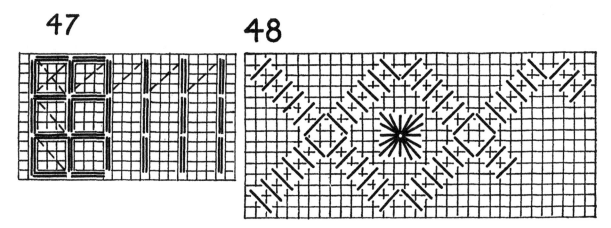

47

48

Italian Squared Ground is worked from left to right and is unique in that it is worked on the wrong side. As the name indicates it produces a square appearance on the front, and is used for backgrounds. It is worked in three movements, as shown in Fig. 49 (a), but before beginning each row, an upright stitch is made which is not repeated. Thereafter the movements are as follows: —

[63]

(I)   The needle comes up at A, down three threads to the right and three higher at B, and up three threads to the left at C.

(II)   It goes down at B, and up three threads to the right of A at D.

(III) It goes down at A and up at D.

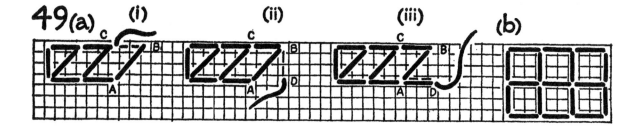

In the later rows the first movement is omitted as this stitch has already been supplied in the previous row. Fig. 49 (b) shows the appearance of the stitch on the front of the work.

(b)   FILLINGS WITH A SENSE OF DIRECTION

Festoon Filling consists of half-circles of Backstitch, with each stitch doubled, and is worked on the same principle as the Backstitch fillings already described.

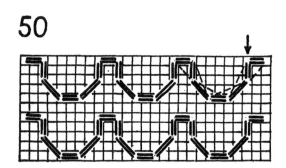

Light and less definite than other Backstitch fillings, it shows up better on scrim than on linen. Fig. 50 shows the direction of the stitches and the position of the rows in relation to each other.

Single rows of Whipped Stitch alternating with single rows of other stitches produce very lacy fillings if worked on scrim, with a strong sense of direction.

In Fig. 51 (a) the Whipped Stitch covers three threads, and the intervening rows consist of tightly pulled stitches increasing and decreasing in length. In Fig. 51 (b) the Whipped Stitches cover two threads and are two threads apart. Two threads separate this row from a double row of Reversed Wave Stitch, worked over four threads. This filling is on a larger scale than the preceding one and is rather less lacy in character. A third suggestion for this type of filling appears in

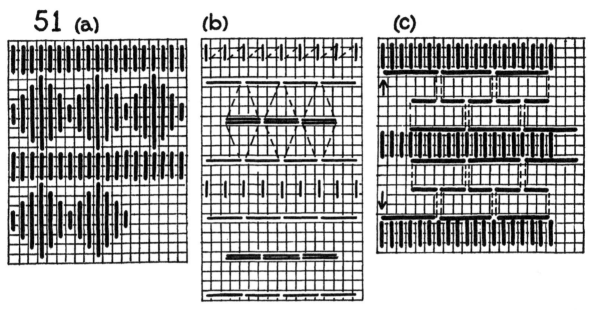

Fig. 51 (c). Here the intervening rows consist of a simple but nameless stitch, whose working can easily be followed from the diagram. Like the last filling, this is perhaps less lacy but is suitable for linen as well as for scrim.

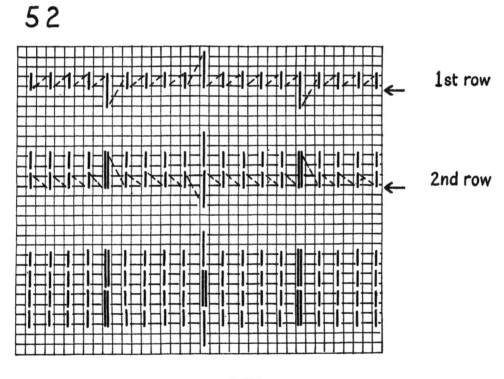

A delicate and charming filling found on an eighteenth century sampler consists of Whipped Stitches arranged to form a wide, flattened lattice, and should be done on scrim. Fig. 52 shows the method. Whipped Stitches are worked over two threads leaving two threads between each stitch. Every fifth stitch covers four threads, the additional two being alternately above and below the line of working. The second row, which may be worked back, is done in the same way; the short stitches are worked directly below those in the first row, but the long ones extending up correspond with those extending down in the first row, thus doubling them. Subsequent rows follow the same pattern.

Crossed Backstitch, or Shadow Stitch as it is sometimes called, can be used for a number of fillings, but it must be worked on fine scrim, where the density resulting from the crossed threads on the back of the work contrasts well with the pulled holes. On linen it is quite ineffective. A simple filling formed in this way is Diamond Filling, shown in Fig. 53 (a). It consists of zig-zag lines of Crossed Backstitch, worked over two threads and two threads apart. The working can be followed from the diagram and requires no further explanation.

Ripple Stitch consists of straight rows of Crossed Backstitches arranged in groups, each group containing three pairs of stitches, worked over two threads and six threads apart. Six threads separate the groups, and on these threads the

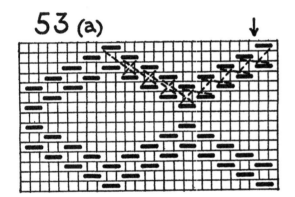

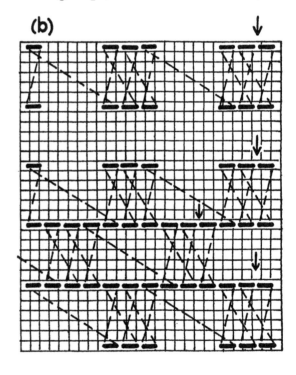

groups in the next row are worked. Fig. 53 (b) shows the first and subsequent rows. Attractive though this filling is, it is not recommended for general use, owing to the long threads lying on the back of the work.

Braid Stitch Filling suffers from the same disadvantage. In this five pairs of Backstitches over two threads and two threads apart are made, and the space between the pairs is then increased as shown in Fig. 53 (c) till it extends to ten threads, after which it decreases to two again. The diagram shows how the rows fit into each other.

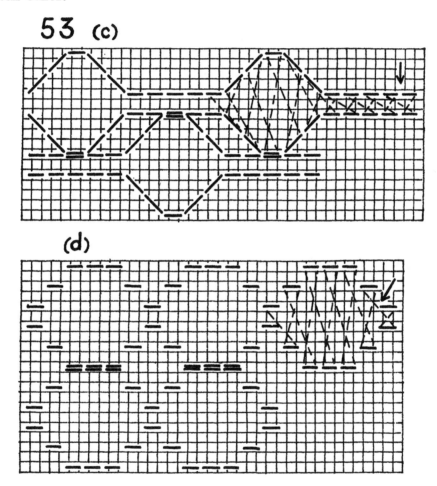

53 (c)

(d)

Cushion Stitch Filling also has such long threads at the back that it is impractical for articles in daily use, but it is included here because it is an effective stitch when appropriately used. Fig. 53 (d) shows its working and the position of the rows in relation to each other.

A delightful filling consists of a combination of Crossed Backstitch and Whipped Stitches. Again it shows best on scrim and has a strong feeling of direction. Four pairs of Crossed Backstitches are worked over two threads and six threads apart, and they are followed bij nine Whipped Stitches worked over the centre two threads and into every space. It should be noted that to get the correct pull for the Whipped Stitches, the lower Backstitch is worked first. In the following

54

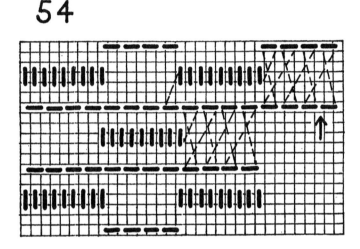

rows the Whipped Stitches are worked below the Crossed Backstitches as shown in Fig. 54, giving undulating lines of holes.

A filling found on an old Scottish sampler consists simply of Cross Stitches worked over four threads. When one row has been completed, the next row is worked so that the crosses alternate or are 'staggered', producing a zig-zag effect between the rows. The position of the stitches is shown in Fig. 55. This is a very good filling when worked on loosely woven material, but it should be tried

55

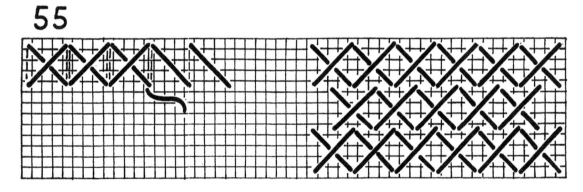

out carefully before use, especially when the linen is not 'evenweave', as it may look well worked in one direction but be an utter failure in the other.

Single rows of Raised Square Stitch, alternating with single rows of Cross Stitch 'staggered' in the same way, leaving one thread between the rows, is a pleasant striped filling on a sufficiently small scale to be generally useful, and is shown in Fig. 56.

56

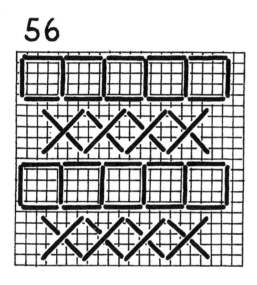

57

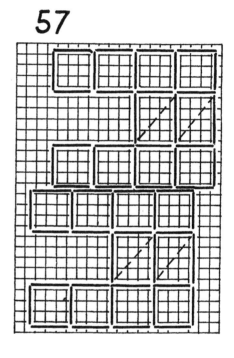

The last filling to be described in this section is on a large scale and may be used either as a border or as a filling. Known as Four-sided Border, it appears in Fig. 57, and the method of working is as follows: —

(I)   Work a row of Raised Square Stitch over four threads.

(II)   Leave five threads and work a similar row corresponding with the first one.

(III)   Over the five intervening threads work straight stitches four threads apart, placing them in the holes made by the square stitch.

(IV)   Immediately below the last row of Square Stitch and without leaving a thread, work another row of Raised Square Stitch, but this time 'staggering' it, taking two threads from one group and two from the next.

Continue by repeating from (II). When used as a border, the final repeat ends with (III).

[69]

CHAPTER VI

Fillings worked diagonally

(a) Fillings with an All-over Effect

A word of explanation about this section may not be out of place, for it may be argued that some of the fillings included in this chapter can be worked horizontally or vertically and that their proper place is in the previous chapter. Whilst this is true, particularly in the case of Mosaic and similar fillings consisting of units each of which is completed before proceeding to the next one, nevertheless experience has proved that the transition from one unit to the next is shorter, neater and generally more satisfactory if the line of travel lies along the diagonal. Any worker who finds it more convenient to work such fillings by the thread is free to follow her own fancy. There is no hard and fast rule about it.

Russian Filling, as its name implies, has the appearance of drawn squares similar to those found in Russian Drawn Thread, and is suitable for most materials. Successive rows of Reversed Faggot are worked till the whole space is filled. Then the work is turned and successive rows of Reversed Faggot are again

58

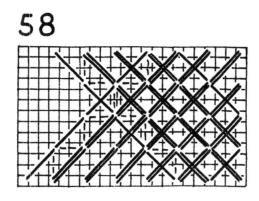

worked in the other direction, crossing the previous ones and using the holes already made. It is shown in Fig. 58.

Detached Square Filling, which is light but needs a lot of space, is shown in Fig. 59, and is worked as follows: —

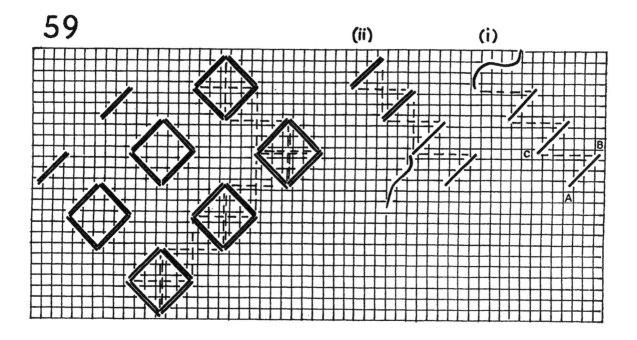

(I)   The needle comes up at A, goes down three threads up and three to the right at B, and up six threads to the left at C. Repeat to the end of the row.

(II) Work back down the row, doubling the stitches already made and using the same holes.

Start the next row six threads to the left and six down from A, and repeat till the area is covered. Then turn the work and make similar rows crossing the first ones, using the same holes and joining the stitches to form squares. This filling, whilst delightful on scrim, is also good on linen, and is one in which colour might be used with success.

Star Eyelet or Algerian Eye Stitch is a light, fairly large-scale filling of eyelets, which, when worked in the way indicated in Fig. 60, is reversible. The needle comes up at A and goes down three threads up and three to the left at B, which is the centre of the first eyelet. It comes up successively three threads down at C, three to the left of C at D, three up from D at E, and three up from E at F, going

[71]

down at B each time. The emergence of the needle at F completes half the eyelet, and the next one is then started by putting the needle down three threads

60

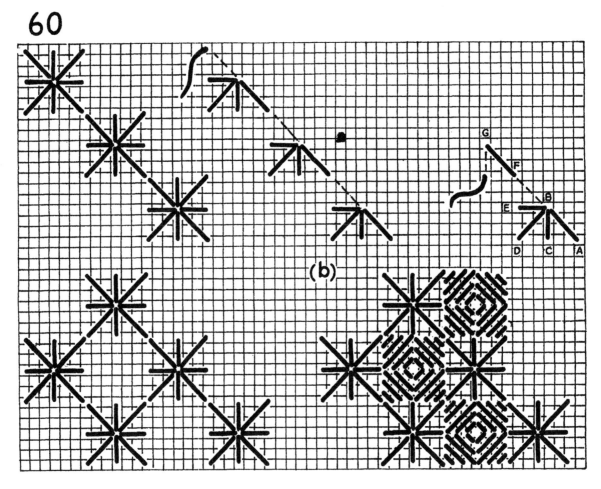

(b)

up and three to the left at G. This is the centre of the next eyelet, which is then worked halfway round as before. Continue thus to the end of the row, then turn the work right round and, completing each eyelet in turn, go back to the beginning of the row. The diagram indicates the position of the next and subsequent rows. A richer filling results if the spaces between the eyelets are filled with blocks of Diagonal Satin Stitch, as in Fig. 60 (b). The Satin Stitch should be done in a soft thread, thick enough to cover the linen closely without being packed.

Octagonal or Oblique Filling is worked on the same principle, but it is on a larger scale. Why it was given this name is a mystery, for the eyelets or stars have six arms, not eight as one would expect. The stitches are longer than in Star

61

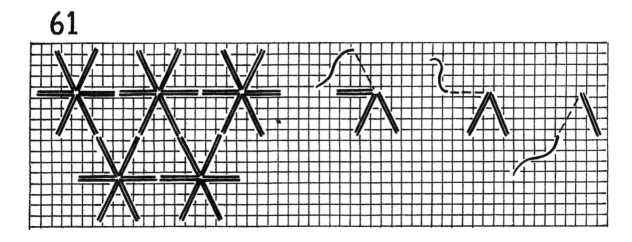

Eyelet, each one is doubled, and the stars are set closer to each other, as shown in Fig. 61, but the method of working is identical, so detailed instructions are superfluous.

An attractive filling found on an old apron consists of a trellis of lines worked as shown in Fig. 62: —

(I)   The needle comes up at A, goes down three threads up and three to the right at B, and up at A again.

(II)   It goes down at B, up three threads to the right and three higher at C.

(III)   It goes down at B and up at C again.

These three steps are repeated to the end of the row, producing alternate double and single stitches. When the whole area is covered by these lines spaced

62

(i)   (ii)   (iii)

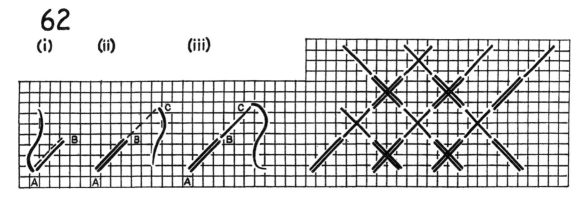

six threads apart as shown in the diagram, the work is turned and similar lines are worked on the other diagonal, forming a lattice.

Triangular Two-sided Stitch, though not strictly a drawn fabric stitch, makes a very effective filling and is, again, reversible. It is worked in two stages as shown in Fig. 63: —

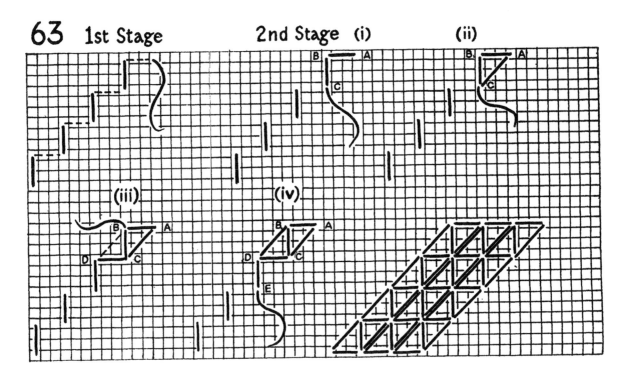

First stage —
> Working upwards towards the right, make a series of vertical stitches over three threads and three threads apart.

Second stage —
> Working downwards towards the left, use the holes already made.

(I) The needle, having come up at A, goes down at B and up at C, forming a horizontal stitch.

(II) It goes down at A and up at C, making an oblique stitch.

(III) It goes down at D and up at B, again making a horizontal stitch.

(IV) It goes down at D and up at E, again making an oblique stitch.

> To continue, repeat from step (II). Successive rows give a rather close, heavy filling, which is good on both linen and scrim.

Chequer Stitch is a lacy filling, with a rough texture which gives it richness and character. The method of working is shown in Fig. 64: —

(I)   The needle comes up at A, goes down six threads up and two to the right at B, and up two threads to the right and two down at C.

(II) Work back by putting the needle down and up in the same holes, giving a line of long cross stitches.

64 (i)   (ii)

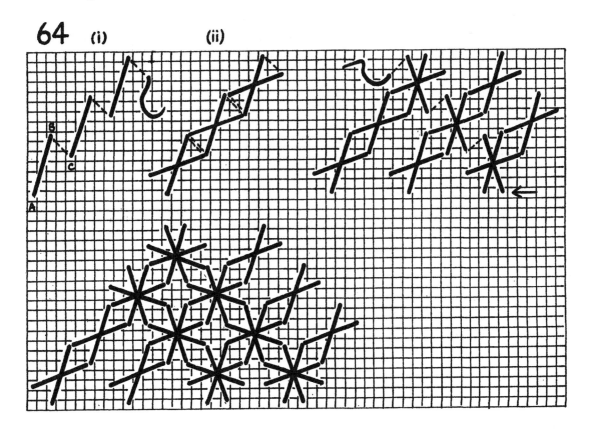

Start the next row eight threads to the right of A, and repeat till the area is covered. Without turning the work, similar rows are made on the other diagonal to cross the first ones, starting two threads to the right of A, i.e. the lowest point of a cross in the first row, and working upwards towards the left. This filling is not so complicated to work as the diagram and directions would lead one to suppose, and it is good for most linen, but is particularly effective on scrim.

Mosaic Filling is made up by units consisting of rows of Whipped Stitch surrounding a framed cross. The working is shown in Fig. 65. Starting at the arrow, work a row of five Whipped Stitches over four threads, and then work three

[75]

other similar rows in an anti-clockwise direction to enclose a square of four threads. In this square work a Raised Square Stitch and then a Cross Stitch, using the holes already made. This completes the unit, which is then repeated

65

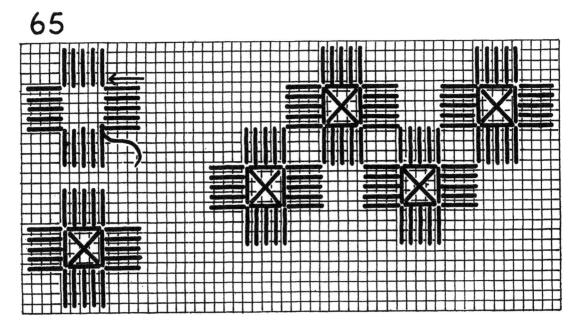

on the diagonal to fill the area. The units usually have squares of plain linen left between them as indicated in the diagram, but, if preferred, they may fit closely into each other.

The units of Maltese Filling closely resemble those of Mosaic Filling, but the rows of Whipped Stitch are worked over two threads only, and the units are separated by long double rows of Whipped Stitch over two threads, worked first horizontally and then vertically. See Fig. 66.

An unusual filling consists of four-pointed stars, each arm comprising three woven stitches. See Fig. 67. The needle comes up at A, which is the centre of the star, goes down three threads up at B and up three threads higher at C, down at B and up at A again. It then goes down one thread to the left of B at D, up at C, down at D and up at A again. It goes down one thread to the right of B at E, up at C, down at E and up at A again. This completes one arm of the star, and these movements are repeated round A, to the right, below, and to the left, and the needle then passes down and comes up six threads down and six to the left to start the next star on the diagonal line. This is a large-scale filling which is perhaps better for linen than for scrim.

[76]

Rosette Filling is usually considered the most beautiful of all fillings, and undoubtedly the alternation of open holes and raised solid squares produces a contoured surface which is unusual and striking. It is, however, the most com-

66

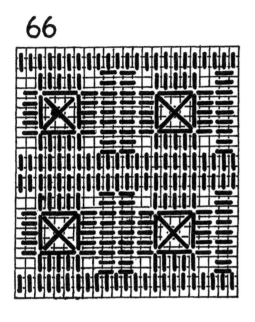

67

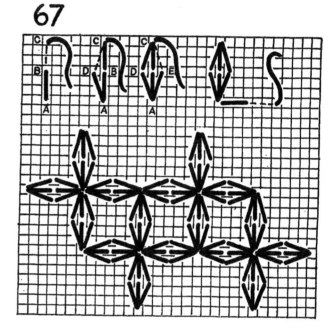

plicated filling to explain in words, though, when the principle on which it is built up is fully understood, the working presents no real difficulty. Fig. 68 (a) shows the order of the stitches and (b) the completed unit on which the filling is based. The corners are worked in pairs on the diagonal in Backstitch, the crosses in pairs on the straight. Each stitch is pulled very tightly, and the crossing of the threads on the back draws up the centre into a little hump, which is emphasised by working four Backstitches round the square. The units follow each other on the diagonal, working downwards to the right, and Fig. 68 (c) shows how the rows fit into each other. As it is probably easier to follow each step in the diagram, detailed instructions which might prove confusing are not given. This is a large-scale filling which is effective on all materials.

Double Faggot Filling, worked so that squares of plain linen appear at regular intervals, is a delightful small scale filling with a close rich surface, which is open to several variations. It should be worked over two threads, and the basic method in four steps is shown in Fig. 69 (a): —

(I)   A row of Double Faggot worked normally.

68(a)

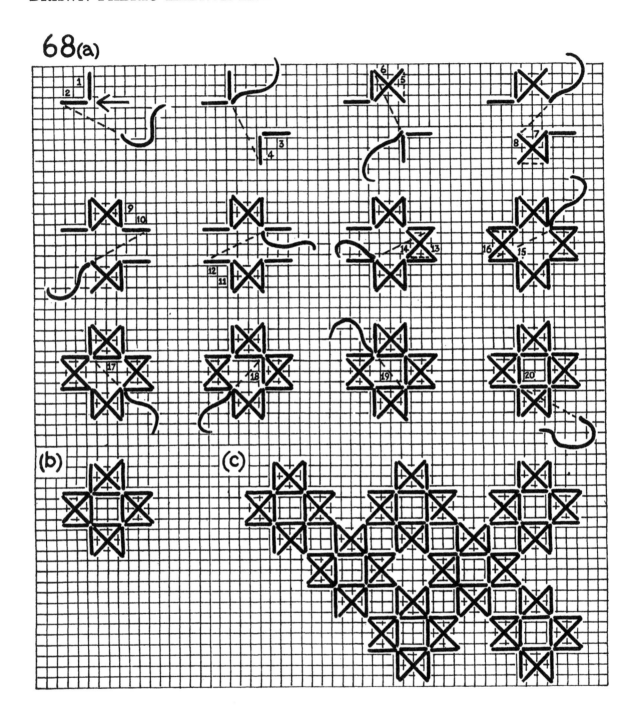

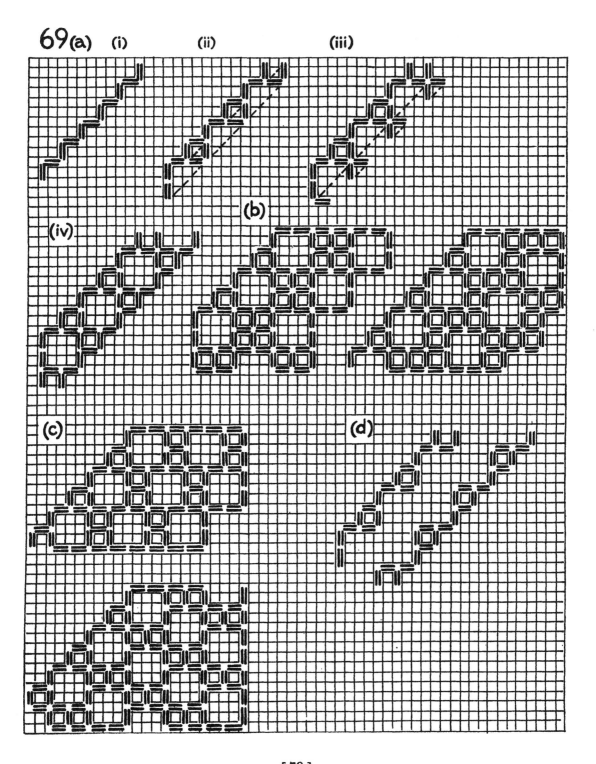

69(a) (i) (ii) (iii) (iv) (b) (c) (d)

(II)   A row of Double Faggot with the needle passing down two steps on the side away from the previous row.

(III) A similar row, but this time with the needle passing down two steps on the side towards the work already done.

(IV) A row of Double Faggot worked normally.

Fig. 69 (b) shows two results which may be obtained by this method of working. Two variations resulting from working the four steps and subsequently repeating from step (II) onwards appear in Fig. 69 (c). A filling with diagonal stripes of plain linen can be obtained by a repetition of the four steps described above with four threads left between steps (II) and (III), as Fig. 69 (d) shows. Workers will find it worth while to experiment further on these lines.

A very close, rich filling, known as Eyelet Stitch Filling, is worked on the same principle as Three-sided Stitch, and is shown in Fig. 70: —

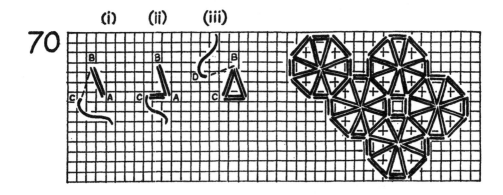

(I)   The needle comes up at A, goes down three threads up and one to the left at B, which is the centre of the eyelet. It comes up again at A, down at B, and up two threads to the left of A at C.

(II)   It goes down at A and up at C, twice.

(III) It goes down at B, up at C, down at B, and up two threads to the left and two up from C at D.

Work all round the eyelet in this way, making doubled Backstitches into the centre, and doubled Backstitches round the circle. Then proceed to make the next eyelet downwards to the right. The circles touch on the diagonal sides, leaving squares of two threads between the straight ones. If preferred, they may touch on the straight sides, leaving diamonds between, but in that case they would probably be more easily worked in a row horizontally or vertically instead of on the diagonal.

Another large-scale filling, shown in Fig. 71, is made up of blocks of five Greek Crosses, worked over three threads, alternating with blocks of Whipped Stitch rows, each row covering four threads. These are most easily worked following a diagonal line, and making the rows run alternately horizontally and vertically.

71

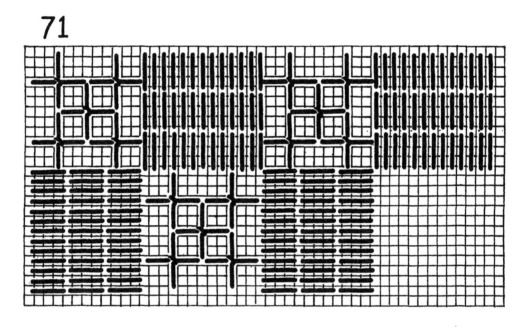

An interesting filling found in eighteenth century embroidery is a combination of Greek Cross and Single Faggot. It appears in Fig. 72 and is worked thus:

(I)   A row of Greek Crosses alternating with two Single Faggot Stitches.

(II) A row of Greek Crosses interlacing with those of the previous row.

(III) A row of two Single Faggot Stitches alternating with Greek Crosses, which again interlace with those of the previous row.

The placing of the alternating stitches requires some care, but their positions are clearly shown in the diagram, and the final effect is alternating squares of Single Faggot and interlacing Greek Crosses. A large-scale filling, this appears to the best advantage when done on scrim.

Squares of Crossed Backstitch may be used alone, but they also combine well with other stitches to give a chequer-board effect. Fig. 73 (a) shows them alone, (b) combined with eyelets, and (c) worked on a smaller scale and combined with small Greek Crosses. In each case the simplest method is to work alternate diagonal rows of each stitch.

Diagonal Raised Band gives a filling with a strong sense of direction and is therefore described in the next section, but rows of it, spaced six threads apart and crossed by rows similarly spaced, make a very attractive all-over filling known as Open Trellis. It is suitable for all linens, but is very lacy and open on

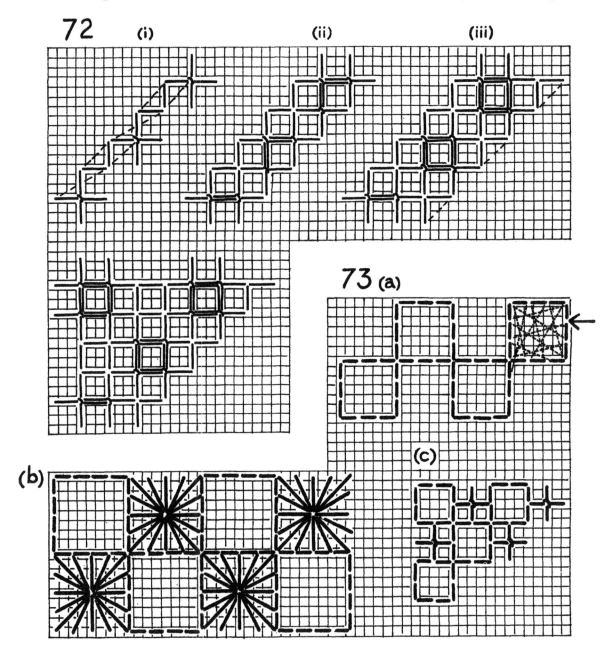

74

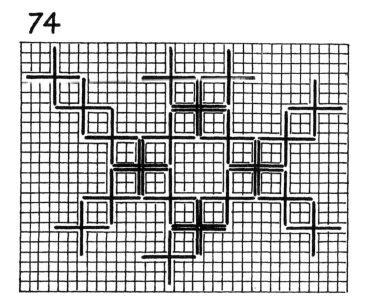

75 (a)

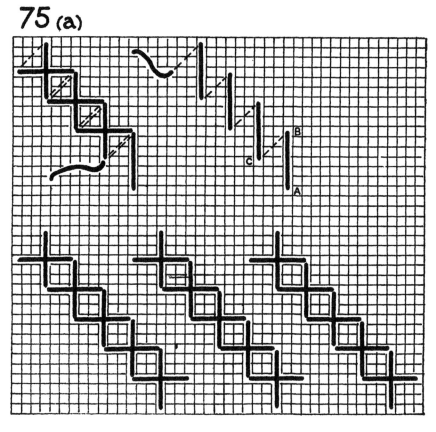

scrim. Fig. 74 shows the placing of the rows, but for the working of the stitch the reader is referred to Fig. 75 (a).

Fillings with a Sense of Direction

Diagonal Raised Band, which has already been referred to, is aptly described by its name, and is suitable for all materials. The bands are worked upwards from right to left as shown in Fig. 75 (a). The needle comes up at A, goes down six threads up at B, and emerges three threads down and three to the left at C. These movements make a vertical stitch, and they are repeated to the end of the row. The row is then worked down, the needle going down and up in the

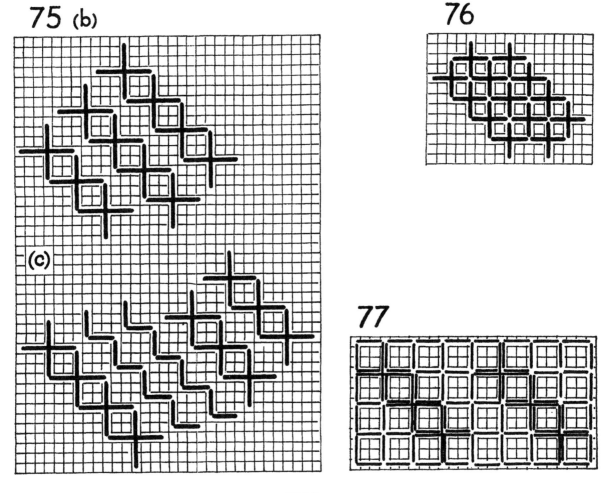

[84]

same holes, but this time making horizontal stitches, and, as all these stitches are pulled very tightly, the material is drawn up into a diagonal ridge. To form a fairly light filling, these bands are repeated with a space of six threads between them. A closer filling results from working each row one thread down and one to the left of the preceding one, as indicated in Fig. 75 (b). Another variation found in old embroidery consists of two rows of Diagonal Raised Band alternating with two rows of Single Faggot, each row being similarly dropped one thread down and one to the left as in the last filling. See Fig. 75 (c). Owing to the difference in the direction of working these two stitches, the work must be turned when the stitch is changed, but the contrast between the raised and flat rows is pleasing and worth the trouble involved.

Ridge Filling, which appears in Fig. 76, is simply Diagonal Raised Band worked over four threads instead of six. The rows are worked successively with no intervening threads.

In Crossed Faggot Filling, the whole area is filled with Single Faggot worked over three threads. Over this Diagonal Raised Band is worked in a thicker thread at regular intervals, either in one direction only, as indicated in Fig. 77, or in both directions to form a trellis, as in Open Trellis Filling.

Net Filling, which gives a very lacy effect on scrim or fine linen, has only a slight sense of direction. It is based on Single Faggot Stitch and is shown in Fig. 78 (a): —

(I)   Work a row of Single Faggot over three threads.

(II)   Starting at the top, the needle comes up at A in the hole already made, goes down two threads to the right at B, up two threads below A at C, down at A, and up at D, the next hole of the row of Faggot. This is repeated to the end of the row.

(III)   Starting again at the top, the needle comes up two threads below B at E, goes down at B, up at C, down at E, and up three threads down and three to the left at F. This is repeated to the end of the row.

These last two steps form small squares, and the filling consists of alternate rows of Single Faggot and squares. Drawn Faggot Filling is worked in exactly the same way, but in this case the Faggot Stitch covers four threads instead of three, whilst the small squares cover two as before. See Fig. 78 (b).

A pleasant variation of Reversed Faggot Stitch gives an unusual filling shown in Fig. 79: —

(I)   The needle comes up at A, goes down three threads up and three to the right at B, up at A, down at B again, and up three threads down at C.

[85]

(II) It goes down three threads to the right of B at D, up at C, down at D, and up at B.

These two movements are repeated to the end of the row. The next row starts three threads to the right and one thread down, as shown in the diagram.

Chevron Cross Stitch Filling consists of two rows of Reversed Faggot, followed by two diagonal rows of Cross Stitch. Fig. 80 shows the filling and the method of working the Cross Stitch.

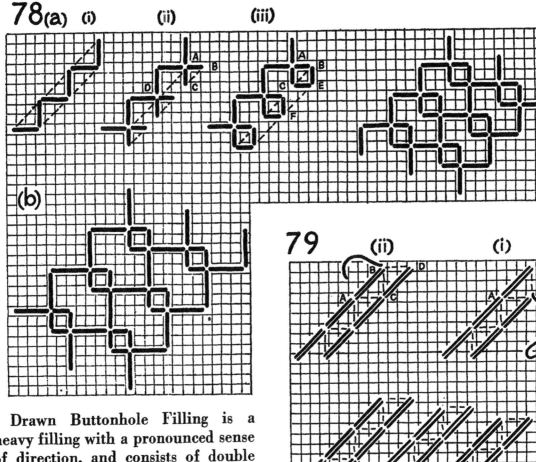

Drawn Buttonhole Filling is a heavy filling with a pronounced sense of direction, and consists of double rows of Buttonhole or Blanket Stitch worked on the diagonal with the heads towards each other but one thread apart. Between these rows the arms of the Buttonhole Stitches meet with no intervening thread.

It requires a coarse thread to be effective, but contrasts well with lighter fillings. Fig. 81 shows the position of the stitches and of the rows in relation to each other.

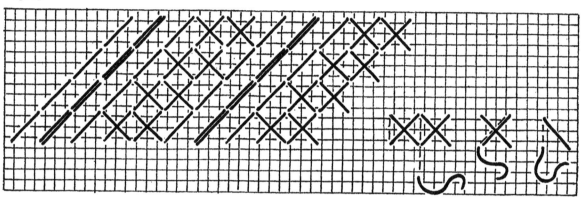

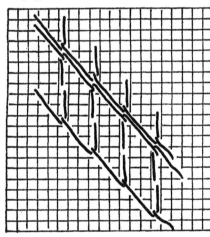

At the conclusion of this chapter it is perhaps opportune to remind readers that this by no means exhausts the possibilities of drawn fabric fillings. The process of variation, invention and combination goes on constantly and will no doubt continue to do so as long as this embroidery remains popular. It is hoped that the suggestions contained in the last two chapters will encourage workers for further ventures.

CHAPTER VII

Additional stitchery

and Isolated Units

Drawn fabric can be greatly enriched by working additional stitchery, sometimes actually over a flat grounding such as Single Faggot Filling or Italian Squared Ground, or sometimes on the plain linen. On eighteenth century waistcoats worked on heavy linen, a filling of massed French Knots is often found with a trail of eyelets, reminiscent of Broderie Anglaise, twisting through it. None of this is worked by the thread, but it forms an effective foil to the drawn work and demonstrates the successful use of heavy knotted work as a contrast to lacy fillings. Such concentrations of knots are rarely found in modern embroidery, but Whipped or Buttonholed Bars, Bullion Bars and occasional French Knots set in little groups can do much to add depth and substance to work which might otherwise appear thin and bare. The centre of a flower immediately suggests itself, but leaves, stems and sometimes abstract or geometric shapes may be improved by these additions. They are meant to be heavy in appearance and should be worked in a rather coarse, tightly twisted linen thread.

Whipped or Buttonholed Bars are very simply done. Two stitches of the required length are set in position and are then closely covered with Whipped or Blanket Stitch, as shown in Fig. 82.

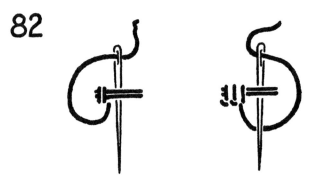

82

Bullion Bars are very like Whipped Bars in appearance, but the method of working is different, as appears in Fig. 83. The thread is brought out where one end of the bar is to be.

The needle is then inserted where the other end is to be and the point is brought up beside the thread, which is then twisted firmly and evenly round the needle in a clockwise direction. When enough has been wound on to cover the length of the stitch, the twists are firmly held with the left thumb and the needle is gently drawn through them and the knot manoeuvred till it lies smoothly in place. The needle is then inserted at the end of the bar and is brought up in position for the next bar.

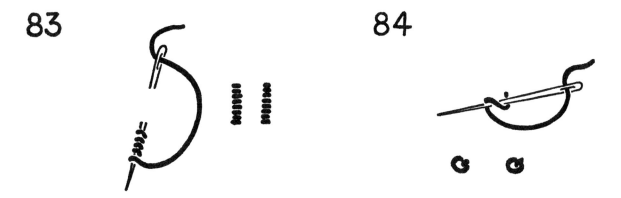

French Knots are more easily worked in a frame, though some workers find this unnecessary. The thread is brought up, is twisted once or twice, not more, round the needle and is held firmly with the left hand while the needle is inserted two or three threads away from where it emerged. See Fig. 84. When correctly made, French Knots should look like tiny beads lying on the material with the thread running through the hole.

Raised or padded stitches may be used on borders or broad stems, but should be reserved for really important features to prevent the balance of the design being upset by their weight. Raised Stem Stitch, Raised Chain Band and Portuguese Border are the most usual ones to combine with drawn fabric, and they are all worked on the same principle. Bars of thread are set on the material and are then worked over in various ways, but without piercing the linen.

In Raised Stem Stitch, the space to be worked is padded with a soft thread, great care being taken that it does not overlap the outline and that it is raised in the centre. Over this padding, bars of hard linen thread are set at regular intervals; they should be fairly close to each other and never more than a quarter of an inch apart. Starting at the foot, Stem Stitch is then worked over the bars, picking up each one in turn as shown in Fig. 85. The rows of Stem Stitch are worked side by side till the bars are filled and the padding hidden.

If it is desired to give the stem a rounded end, the needle may emerge through the same hole at the start of each row of Stem Stitch.

Raised Chain Band is not padded, but as before, bars of equal length are set in the material at regular intervals, not more than a quarter of an inch apart.

85   86   87

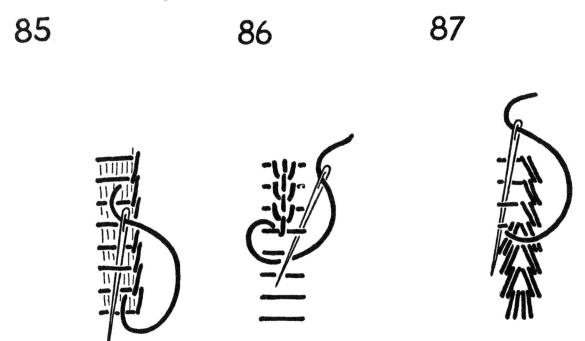

Having emerged above the topmost bar, the needle comes down over it and up to the left under it. It then comes down under the right side of the bar with the thread looped round it to form a Chain Stitch, and these two movements are repeated on each bar in turn. If necessary, two rows of Chain Stitch may be worked side by side to fill the bars. See Fig. 86.

For Portuguese Border, bars are again set at regular intervals without any previous padding, and again they should not be more than a quarter of an inch apart. Having come up below the bottom bar, the needle passes up over the first two bars and comes down under them. It passes up over them again, but comes down under the upper one only, to the right of the previous stitches, and then continues to pick up the second and third bars. Fig. 87 shows the working clearly. For a narrow stem this may be sufficient, but usually the process is repeated throughout the length of the stem or border with the needle keeping to the left instead of to the right, so that, when the work is finished, the stitches form a row of inverted 'V's'.

ISOLATED UNITS

Isolated units vary in size and shape, and their choice is governed by the purpose for which they are to be used. Large ones may form an integral part, or even the focal point, of a geometric design; tiny ones may be set at intervals round a worked shape to soften the outline; the intermediate sizes may serve to break up an area which is too large to be left vacant. They may give finish to the end of a line, fill up and odd corner, or add interest to an otherwise stark and rigid design. These units are all eyelets, but their outer shapes may be square, lozenge-shaped, or octagonal, and they may have either holes or groups of threads at the centre. They are usually worked in the same thread as the drawn fillings, and, as most of them consist of Whipped Stitch, starting and finshing present no problem. The needle is woven in and out of the threads which are to be picked up in the first stitch, and the thread is drawn through till only a very short end remains, which is then covered and held by the whipping. When the unit is complete, the thread is transferred to a fine, sharp needle, and is run in at the back of the stitches. In working all these eyelets the needle invariably goes down in the centre so that the pull of the thread defines and enlarges the hole.

EYELETS

The simplest and smallest, shown in Fig. 88 (a), is worked over two or three threads, covering a square with four or six threads on each side, and the thread

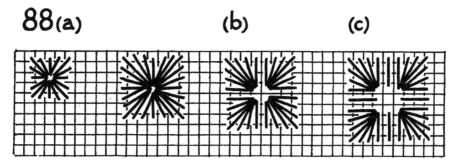

88(a)   (b)   (c)

is brought up in every space. A slightly larger one, which extends over seven threads each way, leaves two of the linen threads crossing in the centre instead of a hole, and each corner is worked round in turn as Fig. 88 (b) indicates. A double cross may be left in the centre, making the square cover eight threads each way, and to do this a single stitch is worked between each of the corner groups as shown in Fig. 88 (c). If preferred, Buttonhole Stitch may be used instead of Whipped Stitch, but the method of working and also of starting and finishing remains the same.

Drawn Square, shown in Fig. 89, covers a square of twelve threads in both directions and consists of an inner eyelet with the stitches taken over four threads and into alternate spaces. This is surrounded by a frame of Whipped Stitch

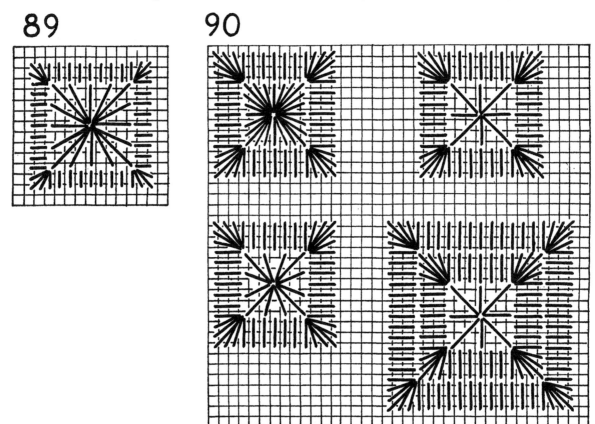

89 **90**

worked over two threads and into every space. It will be noticed that at the corners of the frame five stitches go into one space, which is thus enlarged and becomes a feature of the unit.

Fig. 90 shows other ideas for an eyelet of the same size with the centre stitches worked over three threads, set either into every space or at intervals, and the frame also worked over three threads. Here seven stitches go into one space at the corner. If further rows of whipping are added, these corner holes play a definite part in the design. The idea may be extended, and if a large unit, consisting of a central eyelet with seven rows of whipping round it, has two smaller units, consisting of a centre and one row of whipping, added on each side, the corner holes will be found to make a pattern of their own.

Lozenge-shaped eyelets are worked in the same way as simple eyelets, but the squares they cover are set diagonally on the material, and to preserve the

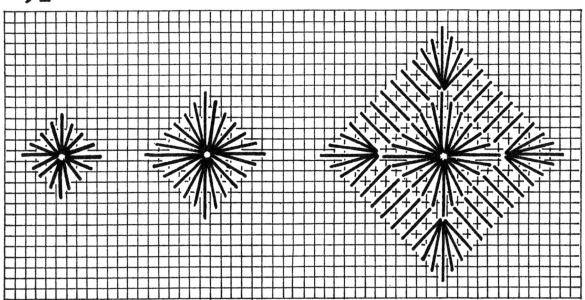

shape the stitches are not uniform in length as Fig. 91 indicates. They, too, may have one or two rows of whipping added outside, and again the number of stitches going into one space at the corner emphasises the points. The size of both

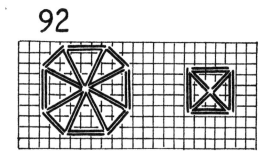

central eyelets and frames is best limited so that horizontal and vertical stitches cover not more than six threads of fine or medium linen; on coarse linen four threads may be enough.

Finally, a unit based on Three-sided Stitch may be either square or octagonal in outline. The latter resembles the unit which makes up Eyelet Stitch Filling, shown in Fig. 70; the former is worked in the same way, but the outer stitches are set at right angles to each other to form a square. Both these units are seen in Fig. 92.

CHAPTER VIII

Outlines

The primary purpose of outlines is to define the shapes of the drawn fillings, to emphasise the contrast between them, and, in general, to supply finish and clarity to the whole. In addition, they serve to conceal the ends of the threads used in the fillings; when they are not used, the starting and finishing of these threads demand great care and skill.

They may be worked in almost any line stitch, provided that it has enough substance to form a framework for the drawn fillings. Open stitches, such as Feather Stitch or Herringbone, are not suitable. Regular geometric shapes are sometimes outlined in Geometric Satin Stitch, worked in a floss or stranded thread, or in a suitable line stitch, worked in a hard linen thread; sometimes they have no outlines. Outlines for freehand designs are best worked in a hard linen thread, wich requires to be a good deal coarser than that used for the fillings, and may range from No. 20 to No. 35, according to the material, the stitch and the scale of the design.

It is wise to have a definite plan in mind when deciding what stitches to use; a haphazard arrangement defeats its own ends and results in confusion. Heavy stitches draw the eye, and it seems natural and logical to keep them for the salient features which require emphasis or depth, such as the more important parts of a geometric design or the inner petals of a flower. If the original plan is later found to be unsatisfactory, and a different arrangement appears desirable for certain parts of the design, a definite scheme should still be maintained, so that the final result is seen to be rational and orderly.

On the Continent, freehand work is most often outlined in single or double rows of ordinary Chain Stitch, with the stitches kept small and rather loose, so that they are well rounded and the line has some width. As an alternative, either

Broad or Heavy Chain may be used with approximately the same effect, except that the line tends to be heavier and wider. Broad Chain, also called Reverse Chain, is started by making a tiny stitch and bringing the needle up further along the line, the length of the chain stitch away. It is then passed through the little stitch, without piercing the material, down at the hole where it emerged, and up the length of the chain stitch further along the line. This time it passes under the chain stitch just made, and enters the material where it emerged, and the work proceeds thus to the end. Heavy Chain is worked in the same way, but the first two chain stitches both pass through the little commencing stitch, and thereafter the needle passes under the second last chain stitch. Fig. 93

93

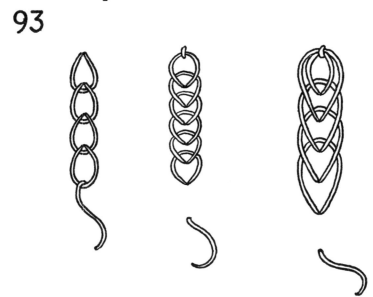

shows these stitches with the threads lying loose to show the working. In actual use they would be pulled a good deal tighter, but not so tightly as to cockle the material.

In this country there is a preference for whipped and knotted stitches, which have a crisper appearance, and, being more or less raised, give the work the effect of slight relief. Whipped Stem, Whipped Chain, Portuguese Knot, Coral Knot and Double Knot are all popular, and to these may be added Whipped Buttonhole, Knotted Buttonhole with a whipped heading and Crested Chain, the last three giving a broader line with a broken effect along one side. Occasionally an outline of two or more threads held down by couching stitches about a tenth of an inch apart is used, but a more successful method, which is often found in old embroidery, is to work close buttonhole over the laid threads with the heading lying on top. Where the line curves, the heading has a natural tendency to fall over towards the inner side of the curve, but this is not unattractive and need cause no anxiety, though in working the pull should be kept upright. Whipped Stem, the finest and smoothest of the outline stitches, is shown in Fig. 94. For this the whole outline is worked in Stem Stitch, which is then whipped, passing the needle through every stitch but without piercing the material. The whipping thread should be pulled firmly upwards from the material to raise the stitch and give it crispness.

Whipped Chain, which is done in the same way, with Chain Stitch replacing Stem Stitch, gives a slightly heavier and less smooth line than Whipped Stem.

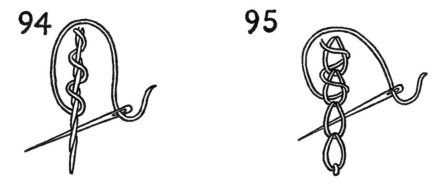

Fig. 95 shows the working.

Portuguese Knot, despite its name, is not strictly a knotted stitch at all, but a development of Stem Stitch, and is worked upwards, as appears in Fig. 96.

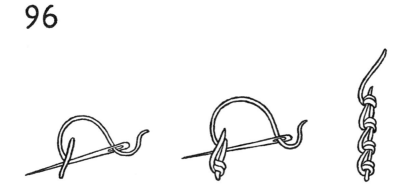

Starting at the foot of the line, one stitch is made as though doing Stem Stitch, the needle is passed under this stitch twice from right to left; another stem stitch is made and the needle is passed twice through both the stitches where they overlap. A fairly coarse thread is required, for if it is too fine, the stitch loses its value and resembles ordinary Stem Stitch too closely to be effective.

Coral Stitch may be worked with the knots spaced apart, but for an outline of drawn fabric the knots should be worked close together to look like a string of tiny beads. Working from right to left, the thread is brought to the surface and is held down with the left thumb so that it lies along the line of travel. The needle picks up a tiny piece of the material in a looped stitch, as shown in Fig. 97, and the thread is drawn gently upwards till the knot is close and firm, and is then laid again along the line of travel.

97

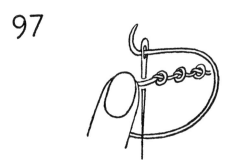

Double Knot, which is also known as Old English Knot, German Knot, or Tied Coral Stitch, is a heavy raised stitch which requires a thick thread to show its real value. Working from left to right, the thread comes to the surface and the needle makes a tiny stitch across the line and at right angles to it. It is then passed downwards under the loop thus made, and, when the thread has been pulled through, the needle is again passed under the same thread but to the right, and this time forming a looped stitch like buttonhole. The thread is then pulled upwards from the material so that the knot sits firmly upright on the line, before proceeding to the next stitch, which should be quite close to the

98

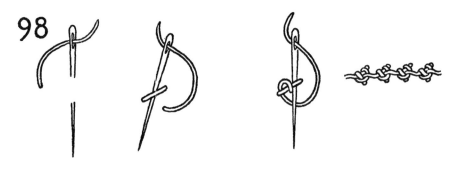

previous one. Fig. 98 shows the movements, but gives no idea of the chunkiness and weight of this attractive stitch. If preferred, it may be worked from right to left, but most workers find the method described the easier.

For Whipped Buttonhole, the whole outline is worked in open buttonhole stitches spaced apart to leave a little gap between the arms. The heading is then whipped, slipping the needle under each loop but without piercing the material,

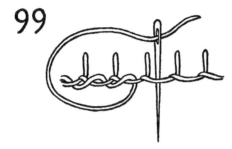

99

as shown in Fig. 99. This is not a striking stitch, but it is appropriate for a broken edge where little emphasis is required.

A more pronounced line of a similar type is Knotted Buttonhole, where each arm of the buttonhole terminates in a tiny knot, somewhat like a French Knot. Working from left to right, the thread is brought to the surface and is taken up, over towards the left and back under the tip of the left thumb. The needle is passed upwards into this loop which slips off the thumb, and the needle enters the material to make a buttonhole stitch in the ordinary way. Before drawing the needle through the material, the loop should be tightened round it and the thread held down with the left thumb till the knot is firmly in position. Written instructions for making this stitch seem complicated, but Fig. 100 shows the move-

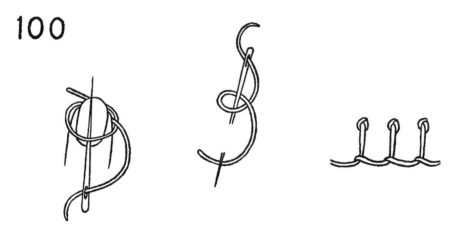

100

ments clearly, and it is quite a simple stitch to do. When the whole outline has been covered, the heading is whipped as in Whipped Buttonhole.

Finally, Crested Chain, also known as Spanish Coral Stitch, gives a closer and richer effect than either of the last two stitches. It is worked downwards as shown in Fig. 101. A small chain stitch is made, then, a short destance to

101

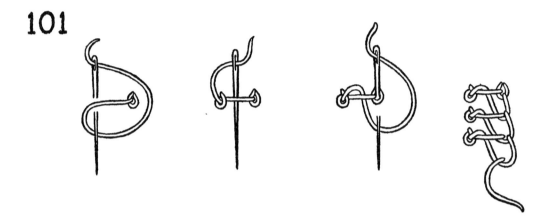

the left and level with the foot of it, a coral stitch is worked. The needle is then slipped under the thread lying between these two stitches, and a larger chain stitch is worked into the first one, followed by a coral stitch on the left, again level with the foot of the chain stitch.

Adventurous workers will doubtless wish to experiment with other stitches, but those described can be confidently recommended for general use.

Plate 6. The corner of a cloth worked on Lockhart's Finer Scrim in eyelets, raised square stitch and whipped stitch pulled alternately towards and away from the worker. The part shown measures 18 by 14 inches.

Plate 7. A geometric design with many fillings chosen to give contrast of weight and texture. Worked on Bisso linen and measuring 8½ inches square, it includes eyelets, raised square stitch, double faggot, composite stitches (Fig. 45) and other variations. Fig. 103 show the edge.

Plate 8.   A freehand design with various fillings, outlines, isolated units and line stitches. Worked on Bisso linen, it measures 10 inches square. Note that the shape in the lower right-hand corner has no outline.

Plate 9. Detail of a freehand border worked on Bisso linen, showing fillings chosen to suit different shapes. The part illustrated measures 9 by 5 inches and shows line stitches combined to form fillings, geometric satin stitch, faggot stitch, open trellis and several outline stitches.

CHAPTER IX

Finishing of Edges

As some workers, especially those with little experience of drawn fabric, find difficulty in deciding how to finish the edges of their work, some suggestions may be helpful. In old embroidery, the edges were often finished with fine close buttonhole stitch in a waved or scalloped line, following the curves of a floral border and set very close to it. The materials in use today do not lend themselves readily to this treatment, and present-day taste prefers that the edges of work done by the thread, should also be regulated by the thread. It is generally advisable then to make the piece of work rectangular.

If hem-stitching is to be done, the hem should be narrow, and a good working rule for all materials is to allow fifteen threads for the hem, and to draw out the sixteenth. The hem-stitching is worked along the space thus left, and this method ensures that the depth of the hem is adapted to the weight of the linen. Corners should, of course, be mitred. A plain hem-stitch is best, and, though this is not often seen alone nowadays, it has a dignity and simplicity which merits greater popularity. The same thread as was used for the fillings should be used, and the method of working is shown in Fig. 102. One thread is withdrawn from the material, and the hem-stitching is done on the back of the work

102

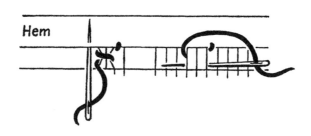

Hem

with the hem held upwards. Starting from the right-hand end, the thread is fixed in the fold of the hem and the needle picks up three threads to the left in the space where the thread has been drawn out. It passes once more under the group to bind it, and then makes a tiny vertical stitch into the edge of the fold, picking up only two threads of the linen. No stitchery appears on the front of the work except the thread binding the groups.

This hem-stitch forms a useful foundation on which to build up a wider border, which would, of course, be worked on the front. For example, one or more rows of Flat Square Stitch (Fig. 6) may be added immediately below the hem-stitching. Two or more rows of Whipped Stitch (Fig. 1) are effective, and, if this is felt to be too monotonous, eyelets of a suitable size may be inserted at regular intervals. An attractive narrow border consists of one row of whipping pulled towards the hem followed by one pulled away from it, and this too may be broken by eyelets.

The line stitch shown in Fig. 10 can be adapted to form a delightful edging, and again the same thread should be used. The hem should be as narrow as possible, resembling a rolled edge, and no thread is drawn from the material. The stitch is worked as described in Chapter I, but the upward vertical stitches are carried over the edge, and are repeated twice, so that the hem is held by groups of three threads. If preferred this may be worked on the back of the work, provided that the correct number of stitches appears on the front. When the whole edge has been completed, another row is worked inside it on the front. Fig. 103 shows the finished appearance on the front and the best way of managing a corner.

103

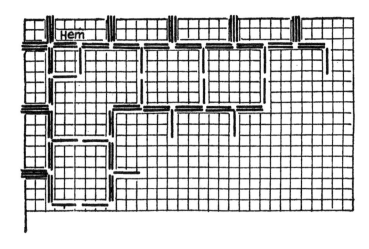

Picot edgings are much in vogue at present, and are both crisp and decorative. They have a tendency to draw up the material, and when being pressed they must be well pulled out to avoid unsightly creases. These edgings originated in Denmark, but their novelty quickly made them very popular with British workers, some of whom have developed both simpler and more elaborate variations. The basic principle of them all is the same; a line of stitchery is set where the edge of the article is to be, and the material is folded back along this line and secured by some form of square stitch or by overcasting worked over and round it, after which the surplus material is cut away. It is important that the stitches holding the fold should lie on the diagonal at the back of the work, in order to secure the threads of the material, and that the surplus linen is not cut away before the stitchery has been completed. The raw edges fray very quickly, and once that has been allowed to occur, the work becomes impossible to do neatly. The stitchery holding the edge is often done as a „stab stitch", and it is sometimes made easier by drawing out a thread to mark its position on the underside of the fold. These edges are surprisingly strong, but if the material is very fine or loosely woven, a second row of stitchery worked through the double material can be added for extra security. The thread should be rather coarser than that used for the fillings, ranging from No. 25 to 40, and all the stitchery is done on the front of the work.

The simplest edging of this type, shown in Fig. 104, consists of a row of doubled backstitches worked all round the material, which is then folded so that the backstitches lie along the edge of the fold. The edge is overcast, making the stitches cover the same number of threads as was picked up in each backstitch and setting the thread vertically between the backstitches on the front of the work and diagonally on the back. When the whole edge has been gone round in this way, it is overcast in the reverse direction, so that the stitches on the front are doubled, while those on the back form crosses. If the backstitches have been worked over an even number of threads, these overcasting stitches may be taken from the centre of one backstitch to the centre of the next, making triangles on both the front and back of the work. See Fig. 104 (b).

A form of Flat Square Stitch may replace the backstitches, and is worked vertically downwards as shown in Fig. 105 (a). The needle comes up at A, goes down three threads to the right at B, and up three threads below A at C. It goes down at A, up at C again, and down three threads to the right to start the next stitch. When the material has been folded, a somewhat similar stitch is worked through both layers, using the holes already made, as indicated in Fig. 105 (b). The thread comes up at A, goes down at B, up at A, down at B again,

[107]

104 (a)

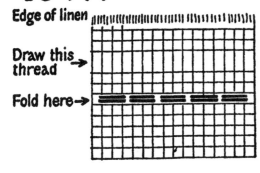

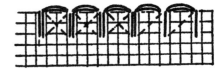

(b)

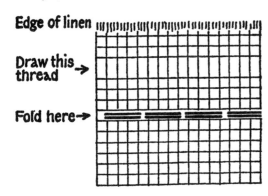

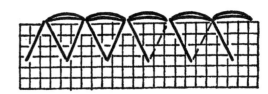

and is brought from below up over the edge and between the stitches lying along it. The thread goes down at A, and up three threads lower at C to start te next stitch. This is a firm but very narrow edging.

A wider version, shown in Fig. 106, is made by doubling the stitches in the first stage, and in the second by working Raised Square Stitch (Fig. 7) with every stitch doubled and worked through both layers of material. As there is no stitchery round the edge of the fold, this is less crisp than the one previously described, and as it is inadvisable to draw out a thread for guidance, the second stage is sometimes tedious to do.

An attractive edging appears to be based on Three-sided Stitch, but the method of working differs from that of the line stitch illustrated in Fig. 11. The first stage, shown in Fig. 107 (a), consists of three movements: —

(I)   The needle comes up at A, where the completed edge is to be. It goes down four threads to the right at B, repeats this movement and emerges at A.

105 (a)

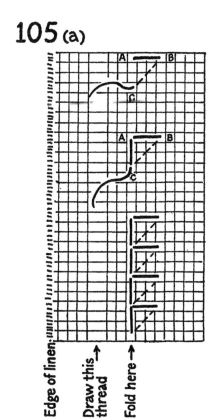

(b)

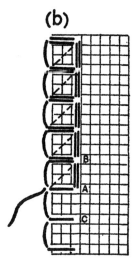

Edge of linen→

Draw this thread→

Fold here→

106

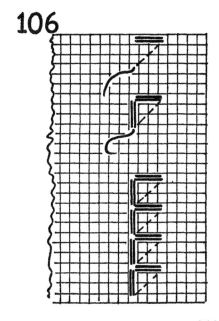

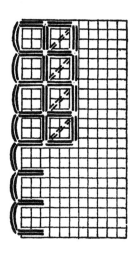

(II)   It goes down two threads to the right and four threads down at C, and up four threads to the left at D.

(III) It goes down at A, and emerges four threads to the left at E, ready to repeat the first movement.

This produces a row of triangles, each with one side doubled. The material is folded along this row of double stitches and the second stage is worked through both thicknesses of linen in three movements, using the holes already made in the upper layer, as shown in Fig. 107 (b): —

(I)   The needle emerges at A, goes down at B, repeats this movement and emerges at A.

(II)   The thread is carried over the edge slanting to the right and between two stitches on the edge, and emerges again at A.

(III) It is again carried over the edge, but this time slanting to the left and between the next two edge stitches, and comes up at C, the tip of the next triangle, where the first movement is repeated.

The original and most admired form of this type of edging has double buttonhole knots which form a serrated edge. It is worked downwards as shown in Fig. 108. In the first stage (a) the needle emerges where the edge is to be,

107 (a)

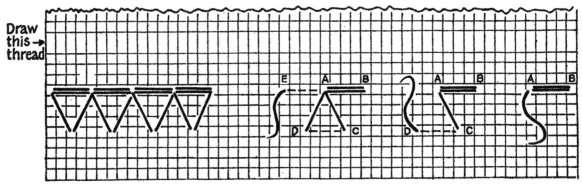

(b)

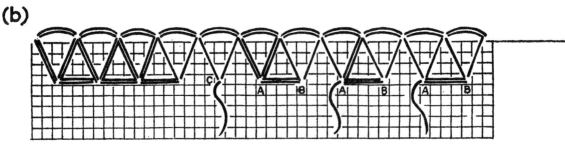

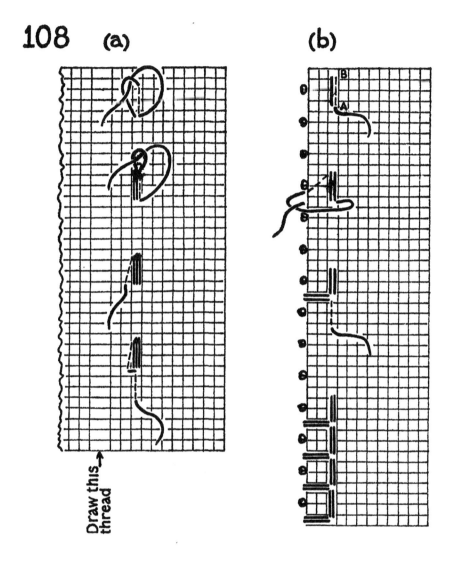

108 (a)   (b)

Draw this thread

picks up the three threads above, but before the stitch is tightened the needle passes through it to form a buttonhole stitch. This movement is repeated and a second knot made. To pass on to the next knot, the thread is taken down at the upper hole, and emerges one thread to the left of the lower one, where it picks up the next three threads in the line of travel, and then picks them up again to form the first knot of the next stitch. In all these movements the thread is pulled firmly upwards, so that the threads of the linen are drawn together and the knot sits up on the group of threads in a way which cannot be shown in a diagram. The material is folded along the line of knots, and the second stage (b) is worked through both layers of material. The needle emerges three threads from the edge and between the knots at A. It goes down three threads higher at B, up at A, down at B, and is brought over the edge. The needle goes down at A and is drawn through the loop in a buttonhole stitch, which is tightened to lie between the knots on the edge. The needle goes down at A and emerges three threads lower down, ready to start the next stitch.

The final edging to be described is an elaborated form of the original one. To work it, three threads are drawn from the material, and those left exposed are buttonholed in groups of three. Fig. 109 shows the method. The needle

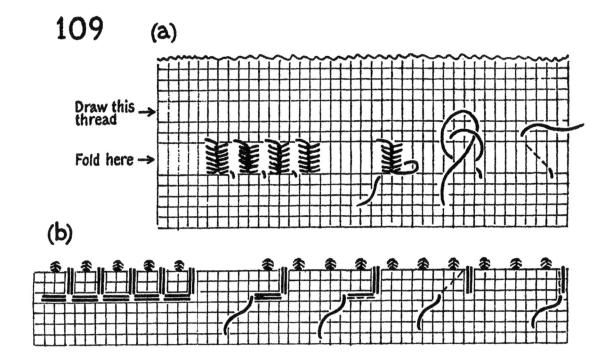

comes up one thread below the space, passes under three threads and across the space, and emerges one thread above it. The three threads are bound together by the buttonhole stitch shown in the diagram, and this is repeated another five times or until the space is filled. The needle is then passed under the buttonholed bar, and emerges one thread below the space ready to start the next bar. The material is folded to bring the edges of the space together, and is secured by a square stitch worked through both layers in four movements as shown in Fig.

109 (b). When completed, the buttonholed bars curl round and look like small beads sewn along the edge, forming a delightful finish to the work.

Of the many forms of hem-stitching and edgings now in use, those described above are the most suitable for drawn fabric. In time, no doubt, further variations will be found, which will prove equally suitable and gain general popularity.

Recommended Books

The foreign books included in this list are profusely illustrated with clear diagrams, and a knowledge of the language is not necessary.

COMPLETE GUIDE TO DRAWN FABRIC — Kate S. Lofthouse

SAMPLERS AND STITCHES — Mrs Archibald Christie

DICTIONARY OF EMBROIDERY STITCHES — Mary Thomas

DANSKE SAMMENTRAEKSMONSTRE — Haandarbejdets Fremme (Danish)

SAMMENTRAEKSSYNING, No. 2 and 3 — Haandarbejdets Fremme (Danish)

SAMMENTRAEKSMONSTRE — No. 1 and 2 — Clara Waever (Danish)

BOTTENSÖMSMODELLER — Sara Lawergren (Swedish)

KONSTSÖM — Sara Lawergren (Swedish)

BOTTENSÖMMAR — Sara Lawergren (Swedish)

MÖNSTERBLAD, Portfolio No. 5 (Swedish)

MÖNSTERBLAD, Portfolio No. 13 (Swedish)

HEMSLÖJDENS HANDARBEITEN, Nos. 1 and 2 (Swedish)

HVITT OG SWART — A. Sandvold and D. Lange-Nielsen (Norwegian)

POHJA-OMPELUA — Sirkka-Liisa Riuska (Finnish)

Index